Helion & Company Limited
Unit 8 Amherst Business Centre
Budbrooke Road
Warwick
CV34 5WE
England
Tel. 01926 499 619
Email: info@helion.co.uk
Website: www.helion.co.uk
Twitter: @helionbooks
Visit our blog http://blog.helion.co.uk/

Published by Helion & Company 2022
Designed and typeset by Farr out Publications, Wokingham, Berkshire
Cover designed by Paul Hewitt, Battlefield Design (www.battlefield-design.co.uk)

Front cover: MC-130E of the 8th Special Operations Squadron, US Air Force, dropping Rangers of the 82nd Airborne Division, US Army, near Point Salines Airport, in the first minutes of the US invasion of Grenada early on the morning of 25 October 1983. Visible in the background is an AC-130H of the 1st Special Operations Wing, which helped suppress anti-aircraft fire. (Art by Pablo Albornoz © Helion & Company 2022)

ISBN 978-1-915070-73-9

British Library Cataloguing-in-Publication Data
A catalogue record for this book is available from the British Library

CONTENTS

ABBREVIATIONS

AA	Anti-Aircraft
AAA	Anti-Aircraft Artillery
APC	Armoured Personnel Carrier
ATGM	Anti-tank Guided Missile
BDF	Barbados Defence Force
BPF	Barbados Police Force
CARICOM	Caribbean Community
CDS	Chief of Defence Staff
CIA	Central Intelligence Agency
CINCLANT	Commander in Chief Atlantic
CINCMAC	Commander in Chief Military Airlift Command
CINCRED	Commander in Chief Readiness Command
CLO	Central Liaison Office
CO	Commanding Officer
CPKF	Caribbean Peacekeeping Force
DIA	Defence Intelligence Agency
FAR	Revolutionary Armed Forces (Cuba)
GMMWU	Grenada Manual & Mental Workers Union
GULP	Grenada United Labour Party
JCF	Jamaica Constabulary Force
JCS	Joint Chiefs of Staff
JDF	Jamaica Defence Force
JEWEL	Joint Endeavor for Welfare Education and Liberation
JSOC	Joint Special Operations Command
JTF	Joint Task Force
MAC	Military Airlift Command
MANPADS	Man-portable Air Defence System
MARG	Marine Amphibious Ready Group
MAU	Marine Amphibious Unit
MBPM	Maurice Bishop Patriotic Movement
NJM	New JEWEL Movement
NLA	National Liberation Army
NNP	New National Party
NSDD	National Security Division Directive
NSPG	National Security Planning Group
OECS	Organisation of Eastern Caribbean States
PC	Police Constable
PRA	People's Revolutionary Army (Grenada)
PRAF	People's Revolutionary Armed Forces (Grenada)
PRG	People's Revolutionary Government (Grenada)
PRM	People's Revolutionary Militia (Grenada)
PSYOPS	Psychological Operations
RGA	Representative Government Association
RGPF	Royal Grenada Police Force
RMC	Revolutionary Military Council
RSS	Region Security System
SEAL	Sea Land Air
SecDef	Secretary of State for Defence
SRP	Special Reserve Police
SSG	Special Situation Group
SSU	Special Service Unit
TF	Task Force
USFORCARIB	United States Forces Caribbean
USLANTCOM	Atlantic Command
USMC	United States Marine Corps
USREDCOM	Readiness Command

1

THE BATTLE FOR GRENADA

At dawn on 25 October 1983, the United States launched Operation Urgent Fury against the tiny Caribbean island of Grenada following a bloody coup, masterminded by Deputy Prime Minister Bernard Coard, which saw the Marxist-Populist government of Prime Minister Maurice Bishop replaced by a Revolutionary Military Council (RMC) led by General Hudson Austin. On 19 October 1983, Bishop and several members of his Cabinet were murdered on orders from the RMC and many civilians were killed in an abortive effort to rescue Bishop and his ministers. The coup and the murders stunned not only Grenada but the entire Caribbean, including Bishop's patron and friend, Cuba's Fidel Castro, and it led to calls for intervention.

Following the violence and murders, the United States and several Caribbean countries pushed for and organised forces to militarily intervene in the island. The diplomatic manoeuvres saw the Organisation of Eastern Caribbean States (OECS), Barbados and Jamaica supporting intervention, while other Caribbean countries such as Trinidad and Tobago and the Cooperative Republic of Guyana (itself a Marxist quasi-dictatorship), opted to remain neutral. This division within the Caribbean community was surprising considering the largely pro-Western orientation of most of the region but reflected deep suspicions of the United States within the Trinidadian government and increasingly hostility to the United States from Guyana, whose rigged elections were beginning to attract attention.

The military intervention was short, sharp and overwhelming. Over the course of four days, the US military destroyed the tiny People's Revolutionary Armed Forces (PRAF) and neutralised the efforts of over 700 armed Cuban construction workers. The result was always a foregone conclusion with the preponderance of force heavily in favour of the American military and with, at best, lukewarm support from Grenada's erstwhile Communist allies. Cuba, for example, provided no additional weapons and restricted the participation of its personnel, while the Soviet Union, widely believed to be sympathetic to the RMC and its mastermind, did little to assist.

Many books have been written on Operation Urgent Fury, detailing the complicated planning process and decision-making processes of the United States government plus the 'challenges' faced by the US armed forces in planning and conducting this operation, but this book will not be one of them. There is more to this operation than its planning and execution by the United States' armed forces which overwhelmed their outnumbered and outgunned opposition. Indeed, there is a background to the events that transpired which needs telling.

While the military operation itself is of interest and will be detailed, Operation Urgent Fury was the culmination of a tragic series of events that saw Grenada lurch from quasi-dictatorship to a socialist dictatorship which promised to bring about a new era of social justice, improved opportunities, access to education and employment and an end to brutality. In reality, one autocratic leader was replaced by another, albeit one who was more charismatic and who was able to accomplish substantial improvements in Grenada's development indices. Yet, that very leader was to prove to be capable of brutality and the subversion of institutions in a quest to consolidate power in the hands of Bishop's ruling party.

However, as will be discussed, it would be entirely wrong to view Bishop's government and its New JEWEL (New Joint Endeavor for Welfare, Education, and Liberation) movement as being merely a Cuban puppet or a wannabe Communist strongman. Like so many left-wing movements, the New JEWEL movement was established with positive intentions: to free Grenada from the thrall of Prime Minister Eric Gairy and his Grenada United Labour Party (GULP) which had presided over the country from 1967 to 1979 and which held power by a combination of blatantly rigged elections, extensive political intimidation and the liberal use of armed thugs. Unfortunately, Bishop's government was to, in many ways, become very much like Gairy's and despite some positive developments, it embarked down the dark road of dictatorship with disastrous consequences for Grenada in general and Bishop himself in particular.

The Significance of Urgent Fury

There is something of a myth surrounding Operation Urgent Fury that sometimes seeks to portray it as a major blow against Communism in the Caribbean, the defeat of Cuban and Soviet expansionism, a military operation undertaken against heavily armed Cuban troops, and a heroic rescue effort to 'save' the lives of hundreds of American students stranded in Grenada. In reality, the students, while understandably terrified, were never threatened, harmed or in any way molested. The Cuban 'troops' were mostly armed construction workers with little by way of heavy weapons or motivation, with the bulk of the fighting being done by the Grenadian PRAF. This latter aspect deserves due attention since elements of the PRAF, outgunned, outclassed, outmanned and completely without a chance of victory, put up a surprisingly heavy resistance and launched three counter-attacks against American forces. The myth of a huge Cuban presence in Grenada was such that to date some less fastidious historians refer to the airport at 'Point Salinas' rather than its correct name of Point Salines.

Even after the revolution which brought Bishop to power in 1979, there was little by way of either Cuban or Soviet effort to destabilise, much less expand, elsewhere in the English-speaking Caribbean which, despite facing numerous economic and political challenges, remained strongly democratic and pro-Western, if not always pro-United States. However, it is entirely true that the defeat of the RMC and its allies in Grenada was a welcome victory for the United States against left-wing movements in the Latin America–Caribbean region, especially as, in 1983, the Sandinistas seemed entrenched in Nicaragua and left-wing guerrillas were destabilising much of Central America and had spread to South America with Colombia being particularly badly affected.

For the United States military, Urgent Fury was its first major operation since Vietnam and its undoubted success was legitimately celebrated. However, Urgent Fury was a hastily assembled operation with forces diverted for the purpose, inadequate planning and a very poor appreciation of the opposing forces. A reliance on firepower, while entirely understandable, meant that there was a degree of collateral damage that still causes some resentment among witnesses to the event, despite the care that was taken to minimise the chance of casualties.

A lesser-known aspect of Urgent Fury, more particularly its planning and aftermath, was the importance of America's Caribbean allies. Through the Regional Security System (RSS), the OECS and the liaison officers attached to the Barbados Defence Force, the Caribbean played an important role in assisting in the planning of Urgent Fury, including drawing up a stillborn plan for a rescue attempt to save Prime Minister Bishop. The OECS was instrumental in building a consensus in most of the region which was in favour of intervention – Trinidad, Guyana and Suriname being the exceptions – and contributed a useful, if largely symbolic, Caribbean Peacekeeping Force. In addition, sustained efforts by the region saw Grenada emerge as a stable and increasingly prosperous democracy in the years after Operation Urgent Fury while the region's courts administered justice to the perpetrators of the coup so that the murderers of Maurice Bishop and his colleagues did not escape punishment. In many ways, this regional effort was crucial in returning Grenada to normalcy and avoiding the extreme civil unrest that too often follows in the aftermath of American military intervention.

Was the Invasion Justified?

Referring to Operation Urgent Fury as either an 'intervention' or an 'invasion' is certain to spark some debate. This is surprising since the words are not mutually exclusive. Depending on the ideological slant of the writer or reader, the US action in Grenada was either a case of bullying a tiny 'socialist' neighbour or a case of saving a country from the evils of socialism and communism. In reality it was neither. What happened was that a government, that was recognised as legitimate, was ousted in a bloody coup which also involved the execution of the Prime Minister and members of his Cabinet. In such circumstances, there were calls for action from among Grenada's neighbouring countries and the United States was legitimately concerned about the safety of a large number of its citizens studying medicine on the island.

The question, however, comes down to this: was there any legitimate authority in Grenada to request an intervention by external forces to oust the RMC? It is at this point that semantics, legality and perhaps some sleight of hand come to the fore. As will be seen, for all its pretentions of being a socialist state led by a 'Vanguard Party', aiming to make a Communist paradise out of Grenada, the governing regime never removed the Queen as the country's Head of State. The power of the Queen, exercised through the Governor General, was fully constitutional and legal, even under the Bishop government and the RMC junta.

One of the more murky aspects of the 'legitimisation' of the US intervention was the role of the Governor General Sir Paul Scoon. With Bishop's government having been effectively destroyed, Sir Paul Scoon would have been the sole recognised legal and constitutional authority in Grenada. While Sir Paul apparently expressed his desire for foreign intervention orally, his request in writing was reportedly backdated to before 25 October 1983. This of course, as will be seen, created a degree of confusion and while much of the furore was moot owing to the quick victory by the US over the RMC, it continues to prove a point of contention in the debate over the justification for the invasion.

The Caribbean intellectual and political elites, whether from the English, Spanish or French areas of the Caribbean, are extremely touchy over the issue of sovereignty and the overwhelming presence of the United States. This inevitably means that any action on the part of the United States, however well-intentioned, or more usually insensitively clumsy, in the region, causes distrust. Nowhere was this more evident than over Grenada and the debate over the US intervention.

In determining the choice of nomenclature, this author has chosen to interpret the term 'intervention' in its most neutral form, to wit, 'the interference in the territory or domestic affairs of another state with military force, usually in a way that compromises a sovereign government's control over its own territory and population.'[1] In the case of Grenada, however, the question as to whether the RMC or Sir Paul Scoon was the sovereign government was the matter in question, the latter making a call, albeit with some debate over its timing, for foreign intervention.

Grenada – A Brief Political History

The country of Grenada consists of the main island of Grenada, two smaller islands, Carriacou and Petite Martinique, and several small islands which lie to the north of the main island. The country is located northwest of Trinidad and Tobago and southwest of the even smaller country of St Vincent and the Grenadines. Grenada is one of the smaller countries in the English-speaking Caribbean and has a land area of a mere 348.5 square kilometres. Its population is approximately 113,000 at present but in 1979, when this story begins, it was around 100,000, falling to about 90,000 in 1983 thanks to the substantial outmigration of people unhappy with authoritarian rule.

Grenada was settled by Amerindian tribes, most notably the Kalingo (or Caribs) who were the dominate tribal group on the islands until the coming of the Europeans. They were responsible for the destruction of an attempt by English settlers to establish a colony in 1609. In 1649, however, the French successfully established a permanent settlement, defeating and completely subjugating the Kalingo by 1654, after which they established an agrarian colony based on the cultivation of sugar cane and indigo with labour

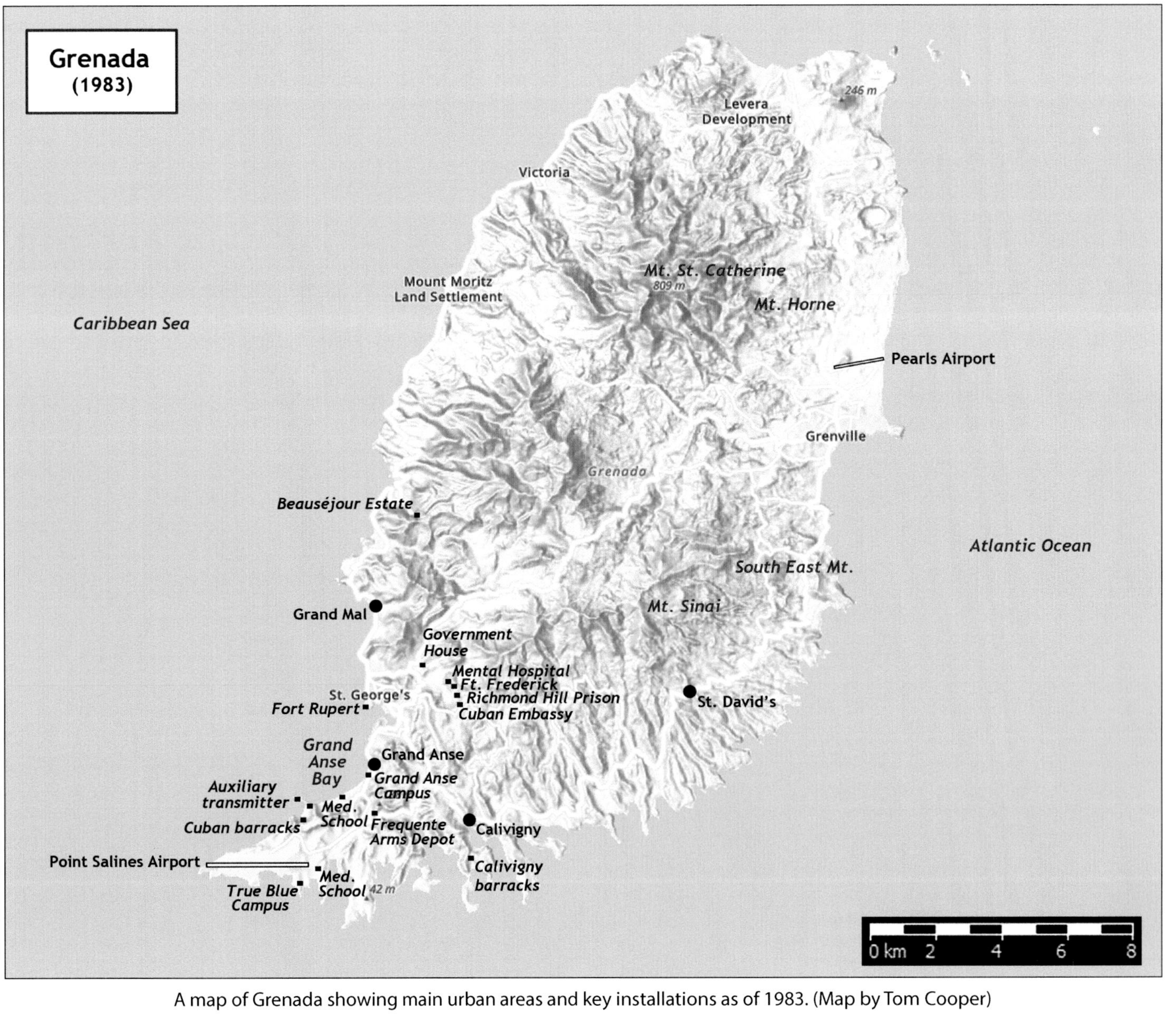

A map of Grenada showing main urban areas and key installations as of 1983. (Map by Tom Cooper)

Eric Gairy. (US National Archives)

provided by African slaves who were to form the bulk of the population, probably by the early eighteenth century. Grenada was to become a thriving agricultural colony under the French and later the British.

The Seven Years War (1756 to 1763) saw Grenada captured by the British in 1762, thanks to their naval superiority in the region. Grenada was formally ceded to the British by the Treaty of Paris in 1763 but the French recaptured the island during the American Revolutionary War in 1779 after an intense naval battle between French forces under Charles Hector, the Comte D'Estaing and British naval forces under Admiral John Byron. The island was restored to the British under the terms of the Treaty of Versailles in 1783. However, dissatisfaction with British rule led to a pro-French revolt in 1795–96 led by Julien Fedon who passed into Grenadian folklore as being one of the first non-white revolutionaries,[2] influenced by the ideals of the French revolution – liberty, equality and fraternity – which found a deep resonance among African slaves who chafed under an oppressive regime. A little over a decade later, in 1807, the slave trade was eventually outlawed in the British Empire, and slavery finally abolished in 1833 with emancipation of slaves being complete by 1838.

In 1843, the British introduced nutmeg to Grenada and this soon, alongside sugar cane, became a major cash crop and the backbone of the Grenadian economy. Grenada became known as the 'Island of Spice' with 40 percent of the country accounting for 40 percent of global nutmeg production. Emancipated slaves still formed the vast majority of the labour force and, increasingly, the population.

Grenada's colonial period was largely uneventful as the colony was small and, while important for its agricultural produce, it was not vital to the British Empire. In 1877, Grenada became a Crown Colony and in 1917, Theophilus A. Marryshow formed the Representative Government Association (RGA) to lobby for greater representation in government for Grenadians. As an Afro-Grenadian, Marryshow articulated the aspirations of the majority of the population and eventually he was rewarded with some success when in 1921–22, the Wood Commission proposed reforms which allowed a limited degree of democracy through a restricted property franchise which allowed the wealthiest four percent of adult Grenadians to vote for five of the 15 members of the Grenadian Legislative Council. Marryshow continued to lobby for greater representation, eventually increasing the number of directly-elected members of the legislature with a new Constitution for Grenada in 1935.[3] In this regard, Grenada was much like other British colonies in the Caribbean with limited adult franchise but this was to eventually change in the post-Second World War period, when there was an increasing push towards internal self-government with full adult franchise.

Prelude to Gairy

In 1950 the Grenada Manual & Mental Workers Union (GMMWU) was founded by Eric Matthew Gairy. The GMMWU began a series of actions aimed at improving working conditions, culminating in a general strike of 1951 which saw major incidents of arson, resulting in the colonial administration calling in military reinforcements. More importantly politically, in 1950, Gairy also formed the GULP and participated in the elections to Grenada's Legislative Council, the first of which under full adult franchise was held in 1951. Gairy successfully contested the 1951, 1954 and 1957 elections, whereafter he was banned from political activity between 1957 and 1961.[4]

Gairy was re-elected in a by-election in 1961 and since the GULP had a majority of seats in the Legislative Council, he formed a government until his dismissal by the British Governor over apparent misuse of funds. The GULP lost the 1962 elections so between 1962 and 1967 Gairy served as Leader of the Opposition.[5]

It was in 1967, with independence for the island beginning to take some form, that Gairy won the 1967 General Election and became Premier of the Associated State of Grenada. Five years later, his party, with him still at the helm, was re-elected in the 1972 General Elections and the stage was thus set for Premier Eric Gairy to become Prime Minister Eric Gairy.

Gairy's first term in government would set a trend that continued until his ousting. He spent lavishly on his official residence without due authorisation and when he was re-elected in 1967, his corruption and nepotism became legendary. Gairy was able to infiltrate his supporters and cronies into all branches of government and the security apparatus while he acquired expensive properties, including at least three hotels, while requiring Grenada's banks to deposit 5 percent, later increased to 10 percent (increasing to 20 percent under Bishop) of their deposits into the treasury which he freely plundered for his own use.[6]

Invariably, Grenadians began to get frustrated with the situation in the country. Agitations against Gairy and the British Governor,

Dame Hilda Bynoe, began to rise with the former working assiduously to undermine the latter. Ever a megalomanic, Gairy became insufferably vain, spending hours in front of a mirror, his apparel adorned with medals. He, like the later 'Dr' Idi Amin Dada, conferred upon himself no fewer than 30 degrees, honours and titles, all of them completely unearned but inflating a vast ego.

Rather more bizarrely, Gairy, while Premier, developed an unusual interest in the paranormal and began investigating psychic phenomena, mysticism and UFOs. This was in spite of his deep belief in his own interpretation of Christianity. He even hosted Jim Jones in the latter's quest to find a base for his People's Temple. Gairy's bizarre antics carried over as Grenada neared its independence, to the increasing disgust of Grenada's people. There was ever-increasing civil discontent among all strata of Grenada's society and soon a new movement would emerge that would challenge Gairy and his dictatorial rule, at some considerable cost.

Independence – The New JEWEL Movement, Protests and the Mongoose Gang

On 11 March 1973, the New JEWEL movement (NJM) was formed. Led by a charismatic young lawyer, named Maurice Bishop, the NJM's political manifesto drew heavily on the influence of the Trinidadian Marxist historian and writer, C.L.R. James. As a political party, the NJM found itself in opposition to Gairy and his GULP.[7] This became increasingly violent in the period leading up to independence. Gairy became increasingly authoritarian and established a police force and a cadre of Special Reserve Police (SRP) loyal to him and the GULP. These SRPs were to become notorious throughout the Caribbean as the 'Mongoose Gang'. The Mongoose Gang had its origins under Gairy's first term as Premier and was established as a de facto party militia for the GULP. By the time the NJM emerged onto the political scene, the Mongoose Gang was well established as a group of armed thugs and hooligans ready to do Gairy's bidding.[8] The Mongoose Gang was often compared to Duvalier's Tonton Macoutes and while there were certainly some similarities, as odious as the Mongoose Gang undoubtedly was, its brutality never quite approached the absolute savagery of Duvalier's thugs. However, their political utility was such that other countries in the Caribbean, in particular Trinidad and Tobago, saw the establishment of similar units (the 'Flying Squad' under Randolph Burroughs) to fulfil roughly the same purpose.

The Mongoose Gang was augmented by a pliable police force – the Royal Grenada Police Force (RGPF) – which had been nearly completely suborned to Gairy's will and which, while usually unarmed, had a substantial stock of rifles available to them for use at times of civil emergency. Additionally, Grenada formed a small Defence Force of about 90 men, all armed, and, because of their demeanour and loyalty to Gairy's regime, they became known as the 'Green Beasts'. Weapons for these forces were all of British origin, with a few American submachine guns augmenting a stock of a nearly 600 0.303" Enfield rifles and a number of Bren LMGs also in 0.303" calibre. Neither the police nor the Defence Force had any heavy weapons nor any armoured vehicles.

As in the case of most small militaries, Gairy's Defence Force was aimed at internal security rather than developing any capability against an external adversary. Together with the RGPF and the Mongoose Gang, these forces were thought to be quite sufficient to deal with any internal situation. With a monopoly on force, the treasury under his control and a ruthless nature, Gairy might have thought his position was secure as the country lurched towards independence from the United Kingdom. The events of January 1974 were to prove him wrong and were to ultimately lead to his downfall some five years later.

The Battle for St. George's[9]

In January 1974, a series of street demonstrations against Gairy's regime took place in St George's, the capital of Grenada. These demonstrations were organised by the so-called Committee of 22 which comprised the following groups: The Civil Service Association, The Technical and Allied Workers' Union, The Grenada Seaman and Waterfront Workers' Union, The Grenada Union of Teachers, The Commercial and Industrial Workers' Union, The Progressive Labour and General Workers' Union, The Grenada Hotel Association, The Chamber of Commerce Citizens, The Lions Club, The Taxi Drivers and Owners Association, the Law Society, the Jaycees, the Rotary Club, the Gas Dealers Association and The Heads of the Roman Catholic, Anglican, Methodist and Presbyterian Churches. Of particular interest is the absence of any of Grenada's political parties – including the NJM – as the Committee of 22 sought to keep the demonstrations away from partisan politics.

Between 9 January 1974 and 21 January 1974 (excluding Sunday 20 January), there were a series of massive demonstrations in St. George's against Gairy, his government and the Governor who was seen, perhaps wrongly, as complicit in Gairy's brutality and the endemic corruption of his government. The protests were largely peaceful with the songs, hymns and stinging speeches typical of Caribbean protests being an integral part of the protests. The regular police, for the most part, did not intervene and while they were armed with rifles kept on hand for such contingencies, for first couple of weeks, no particularly harsh action was taken against the protesters. This, however, was to change when Gairy mobilised his SRPs and armed them for action against the protesters, euphemistically terming his Mongoose Gang 'police aides'. This was to have tragic consequences for the protesters and have a direct impact on the life of the NJM's Maurice Bishop.

On 21 January, about 5,000 protesters faced off against 300 members of the Royal Grenada Police Force (RGPF) and the Mongoose Gang, acting in their capacity as 'police aides' or SRPs. The regular police of the RGPF made little effort to separate the protesters from the Mongoose Gang, the latter being armed with an array of melee weapons including cutlasses, pickaxe handles and heavy wooden sticks. It is not entirely certain how the riot started but all accounts agree that there was a good deal of bottle-throwing followed by an indiscriminate use of tear gas by the RGPF followed then by an inexplicable use of gunfire. The latter was deliberate and often directed at buildings in which women and children had sought shelter from the tear gas. More repugnantly, the police, whether RGPF or SRP/Mongoose Gang is unclear, seized a soft-drinks truck and began hurling its bottles at the crowd, thus beginning a series of running bottle fights between the police and the crowd with many protesters desperately trying to escape from the riot. Police gunfire, it seems, was rarely well aimed and was used primarily as an intimidatory tactic which, when combined with the liberal use of tear gas and the thuggish conduct of the Mongoose Gang, meant that the police were able to gain the upper hand over the protesters.[10]

At the headquarters of the Grenada Seamen and Waterfront Workers Union, Otway House, many of the women and children who had been participating in the protest march sought shelter from the tear gas. However, even here they found no safety as Gairy's police threw stones and bottles at Otway House and followed those actions by opening fire on the building, forcing those sheltering therein to lie on the floors to escape the fusillade directed at them.

The protests of January 1974 on the streets of St. George's. (US National Archives)

continued to amass a vast personal fortune and to reward his key supporters. In addition, Gairy intensified the campaign of oppression and intimidation of political opponents with the Mongoose Gang now more powerful than ever. The subversion of institutions continued unchecked, so much so that at one point, the British, even before independence, considered using force to remove Gairy and pre-empt a left-wing overthrow of the country.[12] However, his reign continued without check by any authority.

However, the beginning of the end came with the 1976 General Election. In this election, which was keenly contested by the NJM, the Grenada National Party and the United People's Party as a united force called the People's Alliance, Gairy's GULP eked out a narrow victory, winning nine of the 15 seats in Parliament. Despite a turnout of over 65 percent, foreign observers termed the election as fraudulent and alleged widespread irregularities, not the least of which was overt and undisguised intimidation of the opposition by the Mongoose Gang. This led to further discontent and unrest and the strengthening of forces opposed to Gairy.

Several movements began to emerge in the United States with the explicit aim of ousting Gairy's regime. One such movement was based in Texas and was led by Mario Marcel Salas, the famous American civil rights activist and academic who seemed to have no link to Grenada (being of African-Mexican extraction himself) but who was increasingly outraged by the excesses and increasingly bizarre nature of Gairy's erratic government. His support would be largely peripheral but was an important step in internationalising the resistance to Gairy's rule. As yet, protests were peaceful but that would eventually change.

Gairy's intimidation of the opposition was nowhere more evident than his brazen attempts to silence the NJM and its outreach to trades unions and other workers. In once such incident in 1977, Vincent Noel found himself surrounded by the Mongoose Gang while speaking to commercial workers. Yet, in spite all of this, Gairy found time to address the United Nations on 27 November 1978 on UFOs!

Nonetheless, the opposition was increasingly concerned by rumours that Gairy would launch a strike on the NJM while he was out of the country. These fears seemed to come true when, on 12 March 1979, Gairy left for the UN, ostensibly to get a full debate on UFOs. Rumours circulated that he had left orders that the final rounding up of all NJM leaders was to take place during his absence. The NJM, however, had other ideas. It should be noted, however, that to date, no evidence has ever emerged to support the contention that Gairy was planning to eliminate the NJM leadership.

At this point, Rupert Bishop, father of Maurice Bishop, stepped in front of his wife and one of his daughters and several schoolchildren to try to reason with the police to allow the women and children to pass out of the area safely. It is unclear whether Rupert Bishop stepped out of the office to speak to the police or whether the door to the office in which he was sheltering with the others was broken down. What is known is that a police constable, with no apparent provocation and for no apparent cause, shot and killed Rupert Bishop.[11]

The riots of January 1974 did not produce immediate effects and on 7 February 1974, Grenada gained its independence from the United Kingdom with Gairy as its Prime Minister. However, the country retained the Queen as its Head of State, with the monarch's powers vested in the Governor General – a fact that would be of crucial importance during Operation Urgent Fury. The newly independent country, led by a mercurial leader who controlled a pliant RGPF and a force of thugs in the form of the Mongoose Gang, was to continue to face sustained internal strife as. the opposition challenged Gairy.

Compared to the rest of the English-speaking Caribbean, even including the racially tense country of Guyana with its attendant complications and propensity for ethnic violence, Grenada attained its independence in particularly glum circumstances. On the very eve of independence, the British Governor, Dame Hilda Bynoe, an Afro-Grenadian medical doctor, resigned after pressure from Gairy. Unwilling to countenance any further delay to independence, the British persuaded a white Grenadian from the country's wealthy elite, Major Leo de Gale, to become Grenada's last Governor and first Governor General. The country thus became independent in the midst of political unrest, a power outage caused by a strike, and a food shortage caused by dock workers in Trinidad and Barbados refusing to load cargoes bound for Grenada.

Gairy's Reign as Prime Minister

As might be expected, nothing much improved with independence in 1974. The economy languished in the doldrums while Gairy

The NJM's Revolution

To call the NJM unprepared for any sort of military confrontation with Gairy's security forces would be a colossal understatement. While some members had received a modicum of military training in Cuba and Guyana – forming the grandiosely entitled National Liberation Army (NLA) – the NJM had no access to significant quantities of modern weapons, firearms of any kind or even proper training in guerrilla or unconventional warfare. The spearhead of the NLA were the so-called '12 Apostles' – Hudson Austin (who had received military training in the Guyana Voluntary Constabulary), Leon Cornwall, Basil Gahagan, Crispin Hypolite, Liam James, Rita Joseph, Ewart Layne, Einstein Louison, Rudolph Ogilvie, Strachan Phillip, Lester Redhead, Ian St. Bernard, Chris Stroude, and John Ventour – all of whom would play a crucial role in the revolution and the government thereafter.[13]

What they lacked in equipment, they made up for in audacity and assembled an arsenal of 16 smuggled M-1 carbines and some pistols, a limited quantity of ammunition, some homemade petrol bombs and cutlasses.[14] They were able to obtain the use of three to four trucks and an assault force of some 24 men was assembled under the overall command of Hudson Austin. Maurice Bishop did not participate in the actual assault but was crucial in its planning and in reining in hotheads who sought to eliminate Gairy's security forces rather than merely neutralise them.

In the early hours of the morning of 13 March 1979, the NJM assault force approached the True Blue barracks of the Grenada Defence Force – the 'Green Beasts'. Of the 90 personnel of the Defence Force, perhaps 40 to 50 were asleep in the barracks at the time and, thanks to sympathisers among the soldiers, the NJM knew that there were no sentries and little by way of security. The assault force threw petrol bombs, setting the barracks afire. This caused the sleeping soldiers to flee with none of them being shot or caught by the attackers.[15]

Bishop's desire for a bloodless coup was very nearly realised but for the conscientious but ultimately fatal actions of Lieutenant Brizan of the Defence Force. Upon learning that the barracks were on fire, he sought to investigate. About a kilometre from the barracks, he noticed a party of armed men on the road who signalled him to halt. One of the men, armed with a captured police 0.303" rifle, approached the car and called on Brizan to 'freeze'. Brizan allegedly reached for his pistol whereupon he was shot and killed.[16]

The police headquarters, located at the old colonial fort in St. George's, was attacked by a team led by Strachan Phillip and succumbed quickly with neither incident nor casualties on either side. Austin's team was also able to easily secure the radio station of Radio Grenada with minimal resistance from the RGPF personnel on duty at the time, with neither side suffering any casualties and with little by way of protests from the civilian employees therein.[17]

The Pearls Airport was secured by a team led by Kennedy Budhlall, the NJM's main weapons smuggler, who then established a headquarters at their home village at Tivoli Junction. This team commandeered a school bus and secured a couple of Land Rovers and then proceeded to secure all of the RGPF's rural police stations which fell without resistance or casualties. Other NJM teams went to secure members of the Mongoose Gang, senior police and prison officials and Gairy's Cabinet Ministers, most of whom surrendered peacefully, with only one Derek Knight escaping capture; he later fled the country without being apprehended.[18]

Bishop had thus secured the country with little by way of violence and, barring the unfortunate case of Lieutenant Brizan, with no bloodshed. By the afternoon of 13 March 1979, it was effectively over. Bishop's gambit had succeeded and the fears of many Grenadians that there would be a violent confrontation between the NJM and Gairy's forces were proved to be unfounded, leading to a profound sense of relief on the part of most Grenadians who enthusiastically welcomed the NJM's revolution. This was all aided by the actions of Gairy's wife, Cynthia, who voluntarily drove to the radio station and made a plea for peace and for the people to support the new dispensation.

Member of the new PRAF on the streets of St. George's. (US National Archives)

Bishop, later on 13 March, made a carefully worded broadcast over Radio Grenada, aimed not only at allaying domestic concerns, but also assuaging fears in the wider international community – in particular the United States and his Caribbean neighbours. In his speech, Bishop indicated that Gairy's former ministers and officials would not be harmed and the jobs, property, families and lives of Gairy's political supporters were safe so long as they did not resort to violence against the new government, seeking broader national unity.[19]

His next words were very carefully chosen as many within Grenada and abroad were well aware of the communist orientation of the NJM and

PRAF troops in 1979 on a commandeered Land Rover. (US National Archives)

its ideological leanings towards Marxist-Leninist doctrine. Bishop went on to assure listeners that all democratic freedom, including the freedoms of expression, of political association and freedom of election and opinion would all be respected by the NJM and fully restored to the people of Grenada, following their suppression by Gairy. He further reassured Grenadians that personal property would be respected and that foreign nationals would be safe and welcome to remain in Grenada, with the new regime seeking to maintain friendly relations with all countries with which it currently had such relations.

The full text of Bishop's radio broadcast is as follows:

> Brothers and Sisters,
>
> This is Maurice Bishop speaking.
>
> At 4.15 am this morning, the People's Revolutionary Army seized control of the army barracks at True Blue.
>
> The barracks were burned to the ground. After half-an-hour struggle, the forces of Gairy's army were completely defeated, and surrendered.
>
> Every single soldier surrendered, and not a single member of the revolutionary forces was injured.
>
> At the same time, the radio station was captured without a shot being fired. Shortly after this, several cabinet ministers were captured in their beds by units of the revolutionary army.
>
> A number of senior police officers, including Superintendent Adonis Francis, were also taken into protective custody.
>
> At this moment, several police stations have already put up the white flag of surrender.
>
> Revolutionary forces have been dispatched to mop up any possible source of resistance or disloyalty to the new government.
>
> I am now calling upon the working people, the youths, workers, farmers, fishermen, middle-class people, and women to join our armed revolutionary forces at central positions in your communities and to give them any assistance which they call for.
>
> Virtually all stations have surrendered. I repeat. We restress, resistance will be futile. Don't be misled by Bogo DeSouze or Cosmos Raymond into believing that there are any prospects of saving the dictator Gairy.
>
> The criminal dictator, Eric Gairy, apparently sensing that the end was near, yesterday fled the country, leaving orders for all opposition forces, including especially the people's leader, to be massacred.
>
> Before these orders could be followed, the People's Revolutionary Army was able to seize power. This people's government will now be seeking Gairy's extradition so that he may be put on trial to face charges, including the gross charges, the serious charges, of murder, fraud, and the trampling of the democratic rights of our people.
>
> In closing, let me assure the people of Grenada that all democratic freedoms, including freedom of elections, religious and political opinion, will be fully restored to the people.
>
> The personal safety and property of individuals will be protected. Foreign residents are quite safe and are welcome to remain in Grenada.
>
> And we look forward to continuing friendly relations with those countries with which we now have such relations.
>
> Let me assure all supporters of the former Gairy government that they will not be injured in any way. Their homes, their families and their jobs are completely safe, so long as they do not offer violence to our government.
>
> However, those who resist violently will be firmly dealt with. I am calling upon all the supporters of the former government to realize that Gairy has fled the country and to cooperate fully with our new government. You will not be victimized, we assure you.
>
> People of Grenada, this revolution is for work, for food, for decent housing and health services, and for a bright future for our children and great grand-children.
>
> The benefits of the revolution will be given to everyone regardless of political opinion or which political party they support.
>
> Let us all unite as one. All police stations are again reminded to surrender their arms to the people's revolutionary forces.
>
> We know Gairy will try to organise international assistance, but we advise that it will be an international criminal offence to assist the dictator, Gairy.
>
> This will amount to an intolerable interference in the internal affairs of our country and will be resisted by all patriotic Grenadians with every ounce of our strength.
>
> I am appealing to all the people, gather at all central places all over the country, and prepare to welcome and assist the people's armed forces when they come into your area. The revolution is

expected to consolidate the position of power within the next few hours.

LONG LIVE THE PEOPLE OF GRENADA!
LONG LIVE FREEDOM AND DEMOCRACY!
LET US TOGETHER BUILD A JUST GRENADA![20]

Unfortunately, Bishop was not to prove quite true to his word. Though he established a working relationship with Grenada's bourgeoise quite early on, he entrenched the NJM and its new People's Revolutionary Government (PRG) into every facet of life. Bishop's new regime, which would have easily emerged victorious in any election immediately after the revolution, failed to seek a democratic mandate and proceeded instead to suspend the constitution and to rule by a series of decrees and 'People's Laws'. Within a few years, any hope for a new, democratic Grenada under the NJM were dashed and in their actions lay the foundations for the fall of Bishop and the bloody end of the revolution.

The Grenada Revolution – A Mythology Develops

Before delving into the grim reality of the NJM's revolution and the PRG's misrule of Grenada, Western readers might find it surprising that the Grenada Revolution has entered the realm of mythology for many in the English-speaking Caribbean. Gairy's oppressive reign became the stuff of legend in the democratic islands of the Caribbean which all experienced an influx of Grenadians seeking work and other opportunities over the decades before and after that country's independence. A large Grenadian diaspora longed for a better future for their homeland and when Gairy's overthrow came, they were exhilarated.

Maurice Bishop became an almost mythical figure to many in this diaspora, with one well-known poet, comedian and story-teller of Grenadian extraction, Paul Keens Douglas, composing a poem called 'Fedon's Flute' about the revolution and the harmony and prosperity it would bring. Bishop was compared to that early rebel, Julien Fedon, and the ousting of Gairy was rightly seen as a liberation from oppression. The defeat of an entrenched government, with its control of police, military and armed thugs, evoked a sense of pride with Maurice Bishop, the underdog, seeming to triumph over all the odds to liberate his homeland.

Ideologically, the Grenada Revolution of 1979 tapped into a broader trend in West Indian academia and in intellectual circles that sought to cast off the vestiges of the colonial period. Many of the political elites in countries such as Trinidad and Tobago, Barbados and Jamaica, as well as smaller countries such as Dominica, were seen as merely replacing white colonial authorities with Afro-Caribbean elites, who were mockingly termed 'Afro-Saxons'.

Underpinning this sentiment was a strong socialist orientation of these academics and intellectuals. This found resonance in movements such as the United Labour Front in Trinidad and in the Trades Union movements across the English-speaking Caribbean. In Grenada, this sentiment was taken to the extreme where the revolution was praised and mythologised to an unprecedented degree. However, this meant that the US intervention, no matter the circumstances, was criticised as being responsible for the overthrow of a 'People's Revolution'. The reality, however, as will be discussed in the next chapter, was that the Grenada Revolution destroyed itself, prompting the intervention.

2
MANNERS TO MASSACRE – THE FALL OF BISHOP

The term to 'manners' somebody is, in many parts of the Caribbean, to imprison, beat or otherwise severely punish a person for a minor offence. By June 1980, all of Grenada was under 'heavy manners'. Arbitrary detentions, arrests and torture were becoming increasingly common. This can be seen in the case of Winston 'Broko' Simon, a farmer and fisherman who was arrested at 10:30 a.m. on 18 June 1980 by several members of the PRA and horribly tortured for several days. He was in detention for 15 months before finally being charged by Bishop's PRG. The courts, in a display of independence, dismissed the charges and the case for lack of evidence. His alleged 'crime' – withholding information.[1] Despite the dismissal of the charges, Simon was sent back to Richmond Hill Prison where he remained until he was freed during Operation Urgent Fury. His fate was not unique. Life under Bishop's 'socialist utopia' was not pleasant, with arbitrariness being the norm rather than the exception. The PRG elite and the PRA could, and often did, get away with anything, and ordinary Grenadians could easily fall victim to the capricious nature of corrupt or sadistic officials.

From Welcome Party to Vanguard Party

Following the nearly bloodless coup of March 1979, Bishop and the PRG were riding high on a wave of popular support. Had Bishop been less enamoured of Marxist-Leninist thought and more concerned with the realities of politics in the Western hemisphere, he would have held an election a few months later to legitimatise his government and to give it at least the veneer of legal sanction. By choosing not to do this, Bishop laid the foundation for his ultimate demise. Strangely enough, despite being a committed Marxist, Bishop was skilfully able to hide this from the majority of Grenadians. Indeed, up to the very end, even after his murder, he remained a hero to most Grenadians who failed to realise that their hero and the PRG were dedicated communists who had frightening plans for the political future of Grenada. This was evident in the manner in which intense political indoctrination formed part of everyday life, with the PRG stressing an elite party membership with cooperation with the 'bourgeoisie' to ensure that a managerial class of sorts was created. This meant that political control was vested in an elite of 80 full-party members, all of impeccable loyalty.[2]

Political control was sought at every level. However, the most dangerous step was the move by the PRG to abolish the majority of existing laws – the legal system (inherited from the British) being viewed as an imperialist anachronism. A series of People's Laws were enacted to give effect to the PRG's dictates. People's Law No. 2 established the PRG while People's Law No. 10 (Declaration and Effect of Laws) gave Bishop, as Prime Minister, all-embracing powers. The most dangerous law was People's Law No. 46, the Terrorism (Prevention) Law which defined terrorism as 'the use or threat of violence for political ends'. Under this law, the PRA or what remained of the Grenadian police, could arrest a suspect without a warrant and detain that person without a right to bail and without trial almost indefinitely.[3] It was under this law that the PRG was able to detain anyone who displeased them, or perhaps who was not sufficiently deferential to the new order. Without either a parliament to debate the laws or a judiciary sufficiently powerful to overturn them, the PRG had full authority to do whatever it wished, whenever it wished. Ordinary Grenadians paid the price.

The Security Service under Lieutenant Colonel Liam 'Owusu' James was tasked with infiltrating every organisation that was even remotely suspicious. These included the church and St. George's University, a US off-shore medical school that attracted many American students. The Security Service had great authority and was answerable only to Bishop, in his capacity as Prime Minister and chairman of the Defence and Security Committee, or to the Central Committee of the PRG. Grenadians were detained without charge or trial and by January 1982 some 183 political detainees were held. Bishop was responsible for approving each detention order.[4]

Indoctrination, the Press and the Rastafarians

In seeking to establish the New JEWEL movement as the Vanguard Party to usher in a new era of revolutionary consciousness, the PRG placed a great deal of emphasis on political indoctrination. Political lectures were omnipresent and began to infect the school system with more emphasis being placed on political indoctrination than on academic results. Despite some resistance from the schools and the strong church – Grenada was and is a deeply Christian country – the PRG was able to establish a cadre of political officers who were tasked with indoctrinating wider society.[5]

Control of the press was considered of importance and one of the first steps that the PRG took was to close down the two independent newspapers in Grenada – the *Torchlight* and the *Grenadian Voice*. Bishop himself stated that:

> When they want to put out a newspaper and we don't want that, we close it down… When they want freedom of expression to attack the government, we crush them and jail them.[6]

The *Grenadian Voice*, in particular, was branded as CIA-inspired and the 26 Grenadians who pooled their resources to publish it were punished, with many being jailed and all having their businesses confiscated. The irony was that the *Grenadian Voice* was aimed at being non-political and operated within the PRG's laws.[7]

While the PRG had some success at indoctrinating school children, with the Young Pioneers being established to cultivate support for the revolution, it had less success with religious groups. The Rastafarians were singled out for special treatment. Branded as 'counter-revolutionaries', the Secret Service alleged they were going to attack a PRA camp. A detention centre called Hope Vale was established for them and over 300 were detained in that facility.[8]

Cuban and Communist-Bloc Support

In the 1960s and 1970s, many left-wing movements – most peaceful, but others much more militant – idolised the Cuban revolution of 1959. Fidel Castro was a hero to many; the darker side of the revolutionary regime not being known to most people. With the Grenadian revolution of 1979, Bishop actively sought assistance from Castro, who in turn was more than willing to assist, striking up a strong personal friendship with Maurice Bishop, and providing political guidance, and military aid. This led to a huge military build-up of Grenada's armed forces and security apparatus out of all proportion to the threats that were potentially faced by Grenada. It is strongly believed that Cuba's influence on the NJM started from 1976. An analysis of the Cuban connection led to the following conclusions:

> 15. It is clear from reporting that by 1976 Havana had earmarked Grenada as a unique target of opportunity – one of the few places in the region where violent revolution by the radical left could succeed. The NJM rapidly became the recipient of the largest share of support furnished by Havana to radical groups in the eastern Caribbean. While Cuba's long-term goals in supporting the NJM

Prime Minister Maurice Bishop with Cuba's Fidel Castro. (US National Archives)

An aerial photo of Point Salines Airfield. (US National Archives)

have never been spelled out either in public statements or in intelligence reporting, it is safe to assume that, once the immediate goal – the NJM's seizure of power – had been achieved, the Castro regime expected to play a dual role: helping the NJM consolidate its grip on power by assisting in the replacement of all political, economic, and social institutions with revolutionary institutions subordinate to the NJM leadership; and using revolutionary Grenada as a steppingstone for the spread of Cuban influence throughout the region as well as in international forums.

> 16. The main vehicle Cuba used to influence the NJM – both before and after the coup against Eric Gairy – was the party's America Department headed by Manuel Pineiro, the chief architect of Cuban subversion in Latin America. Fidel Castro apparently had developed a warm personal relationship with Bishop well before the coup and decided that prime responsibility for Cuba's relationship with the NJM should rest with the activist America Department rather than the bureaucratic Foreign Ministry. In addition to Castro's own direct contacts with the NJM leadership – principally Bishop – Cuba's liaison with the NJM was conducted mainly by the America Department, whose senior representative in Grenada was Ambassador Julian Torres Rizo.
>
> 17. While there is no evidence of a direct Cuban role in the coup by the NJM on 13 March 1979, immediate public reaction by Havana was one of extreme caution to avoid military intervention in Grenada by the United States or the United Kingdom if a Cuban connection should become obvious. Even Bishop denied any connection to or dependence on Cuban aid.
>
> 18. Cuba's overt caution masked a flurry of covert activity designed to secure Bishop's control. Arms and advisers were shipped to Grenada by a number of surreptitious means. Captured documents show that Grenada secretly received a wide variety of small arms, automatic weapons, and ammunition from Cuba during April 1979, while Bishop was publicly seeking Western support. Bishop then announced his turn toward Cuba in early April, claiming an inability to attract aid from other quarters. This began the direct Cuban involvement in Grenadian affairs that continued until the US intervention.[9]

Cuba also served as the intermediary between the PRG and the Communist bloc. However, Cuba's direct, non-military assistance was concentrated in the fields of public health, fisheries, education, construction, sports, and transportation/communications.[10] In the spheres of construction and transportation, their assistance was to prove of great concern to the United States.

Grenada's attempts to develop its tourism sector – the island is extremely beautiful – was hampered by its lack of an international airport capable of taking jet airliners. The airport at Pearls could cater to regional turboprop and piston-engine passenger flights but these were of limited capacity. To this end, Bishop made the construction of a new international airport a priority and sought assistance for this project. Cuba was only too happy to assist him:

> 27. Cuba reached an agreement with Grenada in November 1979 to build a new airport in the Point Salines area of southern Grenada and before the month was out a pilot team of 36 Cuban construction workers had arrived to begin the project. The following March, the Cuban merchant ship Playa Larga arrived in Grenada with heavy construction equipment and a contingent of 136 construction workers, and by November 1980 the total involved in building the airport had reached 300. The total was between 600 and 650 at the time of the US action in October 1983, when the airport was nearing completion.[11]

It is a matter of some amusement, in hindsight, that so much concern was raised over this new airport, considering the larger and better developed international airports already existing in Trinidad, Jamaica and Barbados. One example of the almost preposterous paranoia stated:

> The airport at Port Salines was scheduled to be inaugurated on March 13, 1984. With a fully operational 9,000 foot runway under Cuban/Soviet control, MiG-23s from Cuba and Grenada would have overlapping ranges covering the entire Caribbean. And while in peacetime it would have been used for tourism, the runway also would have facilitated Cuban air support for its 40–50,000 personnel in Africa, and Libyan and Soviet-bloc flights to Central America. Had the Point Salines Airport been operational in April 1983, for example, the Libyan airplanes detained in Brazil while clandestinely ferrying a cargo of military supplies to Nicaragua could have carried out their mission by refueling in Grenada.[12]

This belief that somehow Cuban MiG-23BNs would now be able to target oilfields in Venezuela and Trinidad and Tobago was one of the reasons why F-16A/B aircraft were sold to Venezuela. To date, no documentary evidence has ever been obtained to suggest that any such move was planned by the Cubans or the Soviets. While it was entirely possible that such a scenario as outlined above could be envisaged in wartime, the paranoia over the construction of an international airport in Grenada (one which would eventually completed and named after Maurice Bishop) seems somewhat preposterous but is indicative of the suspicions occasioned by the Cold War and the intense superpower rivalry in the Latin America/ Caribbean region which was mainly focused on only three countries – Nicaragua, Cuba and now Bishop's Grenada. Indeed, even the

United States was eventually to acknowledge, albeit with a major caveat at the end, that:

> 52. There is no indication in the agreement that the USSR had requested military use of facilities on Grenada. During Bishop's July 1982 visit, the Soviets agreed to perform a preliminary survey to establish the suitability of Grenville as a deepwater port. This agreement prompted rumors that Moscow intended to establish a naval base there, but we have nothing to substantiate them. In fact, the survey seems to have caused the USSR to drop the port development idea because of a long reef and other geologic problems, but a captured document shows that the possibility of 'a seaport project' was still under discussion in May 1983.
>
> 53. Grenadian documents on the Point Salines airport show that the USSR had no role in its construction, although Grenada sought financial assistance from the Soviets. When Grenada was running out of money and worried about being able to finish the airport, Bishop turned to Libya to plead for $5 million. His 26 September 1983 letter to Libya leader Qadhafi said Libya is 'the last remaining hope for providing the necessary finance to complete the international airport.'
>
> 54. Grenadian officials envisaged the possibility of both Soviet and Cuban military use of Point Salines. In December 1981 the then Minister of Mobilization, Selwyn Strachan, announced to a Worker's Party of Jamaica congress that the airport would be used by Cuba to transport its forces to Africa and by the Soviets for military purposes. An agenda item of a New Jewel Movement meeting on 22 March 1983 said 'the airport will be used for Cuban and Soviet military.' A Movement member who had received CPSU training in Moscow wrote in his personal notebook, apparently in October 1983, that rumors were being spread that 'the Party wanted Bishop to sign for the Airport to be a Military Base and We did do that.'[13]

This is hardly conclusive of any attempt by the Soviets to use Point Salines as a military base. In fact, a more realistic view was the desire of the PRG to be relevant to the Soviets.

Cuba, on its own, could not provide the financial support needed by Grenada to fulfil the ambitions of the PRG. To this end, Cuba acted, as was noted above, as a conduit for assistance from the other countries of the Communist bloc. However, Soviet support was far less than impressive and captured documents seem to indicate that:

> As elsewhere in the Third World, Moscow emerges as something less than a generous benefactor. The first known economic development of importance came from Coard's May and June 1980 visit. He was promised some $1.1 million worth of agricultural equipment as a gift. The Soviets also agreed on a 10-year line of credit on terms that were renegotiated in December 1982 down from an unknown interest rate to 4 percent. Moscow provided aid piecemeal, drove hard commercial bargains, paid low prices for Grenada's basic export, nutmeg, and made few outright gifts. When Grenada asked on 6 September 1983 that delivery of truck spare parts be speeded up, for instance, the Soviets rebuffed it by saying the pertinent contract had required that bank guarantees be made within 30 days of the contract's signing – and they obviously had not been.
>
> Personal notes and other materials among the captured documents show that there was little if any expectation in Grenada by the summer of 1983 of being bailed out financially by the USSR. While not prepared to underwrite the Grenadian economy, the Soviets did deal with the country on economic terms somewhat softer than those usually accorded Third World countries.[14]

In this regard, it is questionable as to how much the Soviet Union was invested in the PRG, much less the NJM as a political party. The Soviets were never much invested in Caribbean communism outside of Cuba, and it is debatable whether the Soviet Union cared much for the NJM in its early days, extending little by way of either ideological or practical support. Indeed, the Soviets did not establish diplomatic relations with Grenada until 7 September 1979 and did not open a resident embassy in Grenada until September 1982.[15]

However, of particular importance, and later significance, contacts with between the Soviets and Grenada were handled by Deputy Prime Minister, Bernard Coard. The Deputy Prime Minister, a well-educated, ideologically committed and extremely hard-working member of the government, was the most pro-Soviet member of the Central Committee. This was in stark contrast to Bishop, General Hudson Austin of the PRA and others who were apparently closer to Cuba, though Hudson Austin would later come over to Coard's thinking and, perhaps, became somewhat closer to the Soviets. This shows, yet again, the influence divergence of Soviet and Cuban communism in the region.[16]

It is entirely unclear whether the Soviets knew about Coard's growing rift with Maurice Bishop. However, it is probable that they were aware of tensions within the NJM, particularly its Central Committee. Moscow does not seem to have had prior warning of the Coard coup and, just like its Cuban ally, seems to have been taken by surprise by the events that led to the tragedy of 19 October 1983 and had made no plans to deal with the crisis.

Bishop vs Coard – The Beginning of the End

While there had been rumblings of discontent in the NJM as early as 1980, Bernard Coard dropped a bombshell on 12 October 1982 when he tendered his resignation as deputy chairman to the Central Committee. Coard did not deign to attend in person but his spokesman, Selwyn Strachan, played a deft hand and soon, Bishop himself, and his supporters were under sustained criticism from other members of the Central Committee. Strachan's explanation for Coard's resignation offer stressed the inefficiency of the current government, the collapsing economy and that his authority as chairman of the Organising Committee was being undermined. Strachan said that Coard believed that 'the introduction of Leninist measures, including a change of chairmanship of the Central Committee, chopping of dead weight, putting all members to actually do some work on outside committees, and expansion of the Politburo' were needed. These latter points were directly aimed at Bishop who was deemed 'too soft' and who had very poor working habits. Coard had engineered a masterstroke. He pointed out Bishop's weaknesses, noted the foundering economy and had removed himself from any position where blame would attach to him for the revolution's failures.[17]

His bid for power did not require popular support. It required the support of the NJM's party elite and with his machinations, he had the support of most of them. Coard himself had none of Bishop's virtues or vices. Bishop was a charismatic, somewhat lazy womaniser who liked the high-life (he owned three houses and four apartments). Coard had no charisma but was intelligent, competent, ruthless and known for a prodigious capacity for hard work. He was

Bernard Coard. (US National Archives)

General Hudson Austin of the PRAF. (US National Archives)

a committed Marxist-Leninist and ideologically sound. It is unclear whether he foresaw the eventual outcome, but his moves on that fateful day in October 1982 laid the basis for the tragedy one year later – and the end of his beloved revolution.

With Coard's exit, the collapse of the NJM as a governing entity had begun. From about July 1983, the party's upper leadership had virtually ceased to govern Grenada. As the economy collapsed (this, it has to be said, was not unique to Grenada as even wealthy Trinidad underwent a staggering economic contraction in the 1980s, as did other Caribbean nations), the running of the country was left to a few dedicated civil servants who were quickly overwhelmed by the sheer magnitude of the challenge that they faced. The Central Committee spent its times in meetings, arguing and getting frustrated with each other.[18]

It was clear that the revolution was faltering. Membership in the militia was declining and the army had a poor level of party control. Students and teachers were becoming increasingly unenthusiastic with the revolution. Foreign aid, desperately needed for the economy, was becoming difficult to obtain and the promised Soviet and Cuban aid did not materialise. This meant that many projects were left abandoned and incomplete while attempts to boost exports had failed. In every respect, the PRG was failing to deliver on its promises to Grenada. The Coard faction within the Central Committee blamed Bishop for the lack of tangible results.

At meeting of the Central Committee that took place between September 14–16, the Coard faction began the first stages of ousting Bishop and seizing control. Through Liam James, Coard attacked Bishop's proposed agenda and proceeded to accuse the Prime Minister of lacking focus and not addressing the issues. Even Bishop's followers joined in criticism of his handling of things and the overall state of the party. Coard's wife, an even more committed ideologue, directly attacked Bishop, saying, 'The Comrade leader has not taken the responsibility, not given the necessary guidance, even in areas where he is directly in charge, the guidance is not adequate. He is disorganised very often, avoids responsibilities for dealing with critical areas of work.'[19]

This was scathing criticism, aimed at the leader of the revolution. Bishop had lost control of the Central Committee. His still-considerable popularity with the Grenadian population counted for nothing. It was at this point that Liam James played the trump card – he proposed a joint leadership between Maurice Bishop and Bernard Coard. The aim was to combine the strengths of each – Bishop would retain his position as chairman of the Central Committee and be responsible for work among the people and regional and international work; while Bernard Coard would return to the Central Committee and become chairman of its elite Politburo and take over responsibility for all aspects of the New JEWEL Movement as a political party.[20] This illustrates the reality of the power dynamics in Grenada. Bishop might have been popular, but Coard realised that real power lay in the control of the party.

Bishop, understandably, was taken aback and raised some legitimate concerns during the heated debate on the proposal for joint leadership. He rightly pointed out that any such move would be seen as a struggle for power and that the image of his leadership would be compromised. He pointed out that the criticisms of him were 'a clear note of no confidence' and that he could not 'inspire the masses' if he had to keep looking over his shoulder. The proposal, he argued, might be indicative of the imminent collapse of the revolution. In this regard, he was to prove prophetic.

After objections and concerns raised by George Louison as to how this joint leadership would evolve were rebutted and counter-rebutted, the unprecedented step of a vote was taken. The NJM's Central Committee traditionally decided things by consensus so this vote was very unusual. Three members abstained (Bishop, Unison Whiteman and Austin), while one voted against the proposal for joint leadership (Louison). Nine others voted in favour of the proposal. The membership of the party was to be informed in writing, with a subsequent vote on whether to tell the 'masses' decided on keeping them unaware of these developments.[21]

October 8 – Coard Moves

On 8 October 1983, Bishop arrived back from an official visit to Hungary and Czechoslovakia, with an unscheduled stop in Cuba. His chief security officer, Cletus St. Paul, noted that the usual Central Committee meeting was missing.[22] His concern proved well-founded, as for two days, nobody in the Central Committee called on Bishop to report on developments during his absence. Apparently Coard, having received a telephone call from Havana, had learned that Bishop did not accept the joint leadership proposal, and had now decided that the time was ripe to expose Bishop as a 'counter-revolutionary' and depose him.

For three days, until 11 October 1983, the Central Committee conferred at the home of Bernard Coard, who in his capacity as Deputy Prime Minister, wielded all power while Bishop was away. Apprehending the threat that he now faced, Bishop confided to Vincent Noel of his concerns as to how joint leadership could work, while fearing an 'Afghanistan solution' where Prime Minister Noor Mohammed Taraki had been assassinated in a coup by Hafizullah Amin.[23] His fears were very well-founded, as the first steps towards his removal and incarceration were already underway with the apparent connivance of the supposedly professional PRA.

12–13 October – Bishop Deposed

In the early hours of the morning of 12 October 1983, Major Keith Roberts of the Security Service called a meeting of security guards at which they were informed that Bishop had betrayed the revolution and that their primary loyalty was now to the Central Committee. The PRA's party members assembled at the PRAF HQ at Fort Rupert (previously known as Fort George) at 0700 hours in its operations room where they agreed to support Bernard Coard. The PRA party members saw their loyalty primarily to the NJM and not to the country, and they pledged to await the decision and orders of the Committee.[24]

When Bishop arrived for a meeting of the Central Committee at Fort Rupert later that morning, Coard had by then managed to secure the support of the party elite, the military and most of the personal security guards in his fight against Bishop. Bishop's time as Prime Minister was numbered, not in days, but in hours. Wild accusations of Bishop being implicated in a plot to murder Coard and his wife were hurled, these being bolstered by a mutiny of the militia units in St. Paul's and St. David's. Bishop was unnerved by the tenor of the meeting and left.[25]

On 13 October, the Central Committee gathered at Coard's house and the decision was taken to place Bishop under house arrest. A PRA detachment under the command of Lieutenant Callistus Bernard (better known as Iman Abdullah) was directed to take charge of Bishop's security and to ensure that nobody came to visit Bishop.[26] This PRA detachment would neutralise Bishop's personal security, ensure that Bishop himself was disarmed and to take complete control of access to the Prime Minister. This effectively meant that Bishop was a prisoner of the Central Committee and his fate would be decided at their complete discretion.

Later, on 13 October, Bishop was escorted under guard to Butler House to attend a party meeting where some 250 party members had gathered. The chair of the meeting, John Ventour, explained that the purpose of the meeting was to inform them of Bishop's arrest and to seek their views on the situation in the country. Attempts by Bishop to defend himself were shouted down by an angry, hateful crowd of party members. Coard remained silent and the meeting concluded with the decision to keep Bishop under arrest, completely incommunicado and to remove him from his positions in the PRG.[27] Bishop's security detail was also replaced by PRA personnel under Abdullah with the former Prime Minister's personal weapons also being confiscated. He was at the mercy of Coard and his cohorts, but his hope was in the people of Grenada.

It should also be noted that it was not until the 13 October that Cuba's Ambassador Rizo found out the extent of the internal strife within the NJM and the deposing of Bishop. Cuba was caught completely unawares by these developments and when informed, Fidel Castro was livid, writing to the Central Committee expressing his concerns and absolute horror.

On learning of Bishop being deposed, Grenadians began to protest against the Central Committee. Rather stupidly, Strachan decided to announce publicly that Coard had taken over the prime ministership and this led to him being chased away and shouted down by angry crowds. This intense and violent reception led Coard to decide that discretion was the better part of valour and he chose to step down as Deputy Prime Minister with his wife also resigning. Coard then kept well out of the limelight and the public view but Grenadians knew who was responsible and who was responsible for the mess.[28]

Bishop's loyalists rallied the people to his cause with demonstrations taking place in St. George's first being led by an old comrade of Bishop, Kenrick Radix, who was soon imprisoned. The access of the international press to Grenada became ever more restrictive but the intensity of the feeling against the new regime could not be hidden. Shops and businesses stayed shut as pro-Bishop protesters took to the streets with organised pro-Bishop marches becoming commonplace. On 18 October, five Cabinet Ministers – George Louison, Norris Bain, Lynden Ramdhanny, Unison Whiteman and Bishop's mistress, Jaqueline Creft – all formally resigned from their government positions.[29]

Between 15 October and 17 October, Coard and Strachan tried to come to a peaceable solution with Bishop loyalists Louison and Whiteman. They were immediately at odds, with Coard and Strachan justifying Bishop's arrest and removal while Louison and Whiteman demanded Bishop's reinstatement. Coard went so far as to suggest that Bishop go into exile in Cuba and he would permit the protests to continue, evidently trusting that his control of the party and army would suffice to keep him in office. Louison and Whiteman stood firm. Coard eventually agreed to take their views to the Central Committee and give an answer by 1000 hours on 18 October. This was delayed to 1400 hours, then to 1600 hours and finally Coard said that it would be 1400 hours on 19 October. Louison protested and for his troubles, he was arrested and ended up in Richmond Hill Prison. Bishop's close supporters – Radix, Major Einstein Louison of the PRA, George Louison, Vincent Noel and his mistress, Jacqueline Creft – were all placed under arrest. Of his main and most outspoken supporters, only Whitehead and Fitzroy and Norris Bain had escaped the wrath of the Central Committee.[30] All this time Bishop remained under house arrest, under guard.

On the morning of 18 October, a group of party members from the PRA met at Butler House and learned that a delegation from the Central Committee, including Hudson Austin, would put the final proposals from the Committee to Bishop. If he failed to accept them, then martial law would be imposed. While Abdullah was entirely in favour of imposing martial law immediately, the other officers of the PRA were far more circumspect. Despite the loyalty of the PRA, the officer corps had reservations as to whether it would be willing or able to impose military rule on the population.[31]

The next day, 19 October 1983, would be a fateful one. Ventour instructed all civilian party members to report there by 0700 hours.[32] What he did not envisage – what none of the Central Committee envisaged – was that Bishop was personally popular. He *was*, for the average Grenadian, the Revolution. The Central Committee was neither popular not particularly competent and as such there was little by way of connection with the masses. Keeping Bishop incommunicado did not help either as he could not calm down the crowds. Yet, what happened that infamous day would go down in Caribbean history as 'Bloody Wednesday'.

Bloody Wednesday: The End of the Grenada Revolution

Whiteman had continued to whip up the Grenadian people and he persuaded them to march to Bishop's house with the explicit aim of rescuing the Prime Minister. The crowd built from a strength of hundreds to thousands who assembled in Market Square. Led by Whiteman, Fitzroy Bain and Vincent Noel, the crowd began chanting, 'We want Maurice, we want Maurice'.[33] As the crowd increased, Coard and his supporters realised the potential danger of the situation. Though they all carried pistols, the Coard supporters sought the support of the PRA. Layne then telephoned the duty officer at Fort Frederick and made the ultimately fateful decision to request the dispatch of three BTR-60 APCS; they were duly dispatched and arrived on site by 1000 hours under the command of PRA Major Gahagan.

As Bishop's and Coard's respective houses were next to each other, these APCs had to force their way through the crowd but took no threatening action, with the crews and troops fraternising with the crowds. Two of the BTRs got as far as Coard's house, the other being left behind. Abdullah, at Bishop's house, had deployed his men at the gates where they were pushing back crowds who were trying to enter to rescue Bishop and his mistress, Jacqueline Creft. Abdullah was reluctant to open fire on the crowd, at the time, and sought the timely intervention of Major Gahagan.[34]

However, things were not that simple for Coard. He realised that hate was emanating from the crowd and that it was directed at him and, more importantly, that his own life was in jeopardy. Layne could not be sure of the loyalty of the APC crews and the mounted troops which, while members of the motorised company, were not necessarily supporters of the Central Committee and had been detailed as being the first available troops. Layne unsuccessfully sought to get to Bishop's house to speak to him and try to arrange a compromise or at least to diffuse the tense atmosphere.

It was at this point that Abdullah, under severe pressure, realised that he could not control the crowd outside Bishop's house without a recourse to violence. Arming himself with a M3 'Grease Gun', he fired two short bursts into the air, hoping to deter the crowd. Gahagan, on noticing this, instructed the gunners of the BTRs to fire into the air with their turret-mounted 14.5mm KPV machine guns. Two long bursts from those weapons temporarily silenced the crowd but soon they were shouting 'Shoot us. Kill us' and they swept past Abdullah's troops and secured the house, freeing Bishop and Creft.[35]

Freed by the crowds at about 1000 hours on 19 October, Bishop was in a weakened state. However, he seemed to be on the brink of salvaging his situation and winning against Coard. The PRA troops had not shown any inclination to fire on the crowd but Bishop was understandably now very distrustful of the PRA.[36] Unfortunately, despite the proximity, Bishop failed to take advantage of the situation to arrest or otherwise neutralise Coard and his cohorts who were easily within his grasp. This failure to arrest Coard and his supporters was ultimately to cost Bishop and many others their lives.

Bishop joined a massive crowd for an entry into St. George's. However, instead of going to Market Square where his followers had gathered in large numbers, he decided to go to Fort Rupert. From a certain point of view, this made sense as at the fort, as legitimate commander of the PRAF, he could rally the PRAF to his cause and there he had access to supplies, weapons and communications gear. He could therefore gather his strength and resources for the struggle ahead. If Fort Rupert could be taken without a fight, his decision would make sense and was completely reasonable.

Along the way to Fort Rupert, Bishop's side made an appeal to the Cubans to assist. However, Ambassador Rizo lacked the authority to take such a decision. He contacted Havana for instructions but, after an hour, he was told that under no circumstances were the Cubans to intervene in local Grenadian turmoil. As such, Bishop's friend and ally, Fidel Castro, deprived Bishop of the only armed force – the Cuban military and civilian personnel on the island – who might have deterred Coard and his supporters in the PRAF from taking the course of action upon which they were ultimately to embark.

Bishop's gambit, however, seemed to pay off. Despite being alerted to Bishop's release and being fully aware of the shifting balance of power, the PRA garrison at Fort Rupert, led by Major Chris Stroude, was at a loss of what to do. Captain Redhead was dispatched to find tear gas rounds and fire trucks to ensure that non-lethal means were available to disperse the crowds and offer the 60 PRA personnel in the fort a degree of protection from Bishop's supporters. In the event, the fire trucks were unavailable and despite Redhead's best efforts, tear gas did not arrive on time.[37]

Fort Rupert fell to Bishop's supporters without a shot being fired in its defence. Bishop and his supporters quickly took control of most of the installation and Major Einstein Louison was placed in command of the PRA and ordered to distribute arms to Bishop's supporters. The PRA garrison and its leaders were not forcibly disarmed but stowed their weapons in an armourer's tunnel where they could be easily accessed. Communications were established as best they could, and Coard's communications with Fort Frederick were cut off. By 1300 hours, Fort Rupert was secured. However, Bishop had not reckoned with the motorised company.

Fort Frederick was the headquarters of Military Region 1 and the home of Second Lieutenant Raeburn Nelson's motorised company with two of its platoons mounted in BTR-60 APCs. Officer Cadet Mayers sounded the alarm (banging on an old piece of iron) and assembled the troops available to the company. He also informed them that Bishop and his supporters were trying to 'turn back the Revolution' and that they would have to retake Fort Rupert. He was able to assemble a platoon of 25 men in full combat gear in three APCs. Meanwhile, Coard, Austin, Layne and others assembled to plan.[38]

Coard and company planned for Bishop and his colleagues to be killed in the fighting to retake Fort Rupert and intended to spread the canard that Bishop had been freed by 'counterrevolutionaries and big businessmen'. With this, they hoped that Bishop would be painted in a negative light, their own actions to remove him justified and the actions by the PRA to retake their own headquarters, though it resulted in deaths, would be explained and excused by the resistance offered by Bishop and his supporters. If they failed, there would be no mercy shown. It was Bishop's life or theirs.[39]

Though Second Lieutenant Nelson was the commander of the motorised company, he was relegated to a supporting role in the third APC. Officer Cadet Mayers, nominally commander of the PRA's mobile company, was placed in overall command in the lead APC because he had spent time serving in the US Army. Lieutenant Iman Abdullah, of Bishop's guard detachment, was in the second APC and had been chosen for his ruthless streak and his political reliability. Of the three officers, Nelson, the ostensible commander of the motorised company, was deemed the least politically reliable; this, perhaps, ultimately acquitting him of murder.[40]

With the troops in each vehicle armed with a mix of AKMs, PKM and RPK machine guns and RPGs, (plus Abdullah's M3) the column

Civilians fleeing the attack on Fort Rupert, passing by a BTR-60. (US National Archives)

of three APCs moved towards Fort Rupert.[41] The pro-Bishop crowd did not realise the intent of the vehicles, thinking that the PRA was still loyal to Bishop. This did not change when the troops of Abdullah's and Mayers's APCs dismounted and moved to support their respective vehicles as they approached the largely open path to Fort Rupert. Crowds had thronged the balcony of the first floor and few of the people had weapons.

At this point, one of the soldiers in the column fired an RPG as a signal. His shot went low, destroying a vehicle. Mayers instructed his troops and his APC to concentrate fire on the fort and the 14.5mm machine gun opened fire accordingly, with the gunner raking the crowd and the buildings. Abdullah's APC joined in the carnage with the dismounted troops from both APCs beginning firing at the fort and the people therein, with the RPG adding its weight to the fire. It was a massacre of civilians, with the thin walls of the fort offering little protection.[42]

Bishop was heard to exclaim, 'Oh God, oh God! They've turned their guns on the masses'. The firing by the attacking soldiers continued without respite but by now the few among Bishop's supporters who were armed began to shoot back. Despite the disparity in firepower, they took a toll when Mayers was shot in the groin and subsequently died. Warrant Officer Raphael Mason was killed while advancing towards the fort while Lance Corporal Martin Simon was also killed. In return, the attackers had killed between 30 and 40, mainly unarmed civilians and over a hundred others were treated for wounds.[43]

This unequal struggle could not last. After 10 minutes, those inside the operations room of Fort Rupert surrendered to Abdullah, who was now commanding the attacking troops. Surprisingly, most of the pro-Bishop faction managed to escape injury, with Bishop, Whiteman, Creft and Norris Bain being taken into custody.[44] The PRA troops who had been disarmed when Fort Rupert had been taken by Bishop, re-armed themselves with Sergeant Fabian Gabriel being particularly fortunate as he was recognised as a fellow soldier while two others with him, not being PRA personnel, were deemed to be pro-Bishop sympathisers and treated with scant courtesy or respect.

Major Stroude and his men emerged from shelter to take their revenge. They joined Abdullah's forces and subsequently reassumed control of Fort Rupert. In custody were Bishop, Creft, Whiteman, Norris and Fitzroy Bain and one of Bishop's friends, 'Brat' Bullen. Two others, Maitland and Hayling, soon joined them. Redhead took charge of the situation and, with a series of choice abuses, had the seven men and one woman lined up, preparing to execute them. The men were ordered to remove their shirts, an indignity not visited upon Creft.[45] One of Bishop's supporters escaped – Major Louison – injured, he was later imprisoned.

Deciding how to execute Bishop and his colleagues was now the problem. The plan to have them killed for the battle for Fort Rupert was a failure. Leaving the prisoners for nearly 45 minutes against a wall, Abdullah and Redhead sought instructions from the Central Committee. The decision in favour of executing the eight prisoners was taken at about 1400 hours. All accounts say that the prisoners showed no emotional breakdown. Bishop, a chain smoker, requested a light for a cigarette but was viciously denied this final courtesy.[46] Their fate was inevitable yet they met it with dignity under the trying circumstances.

At about a minute after 1400 hours, Abdullah, with his M3, positioned himself in the centre of the three executioners – the other two being Privates Cosmos Richardson and Andy Mitchell armed with belt-fed PKM machine guns.[47] Corporal Vincent Joseph was prone with a third PKM. Abdullah read out the decision of the Central Committee and despite a brief plea from Creft that she was pregnant, the command to open fire was given.[48] The three machine guns and Abdullah's M3 cut down the helpless prisoners. After a minute, the firing ceased. Sergeant Fabian Gabriel said: 'Bodies tripe open. Fitzroy Bain tripe was out, Maurice Bishop back, belly and neck was cut, Jacqueline Creft hand fly off. The bodies were lying there, virtually cut in bits and blood. Pieces of flesh of the bodies were also stuck on the wall'.[49]

Bishop and seven others lay dead.

3
THE REACTION OF THE REGION AND THE INTERNATIONAL COMMUNITY

As will be detailed later, by the time Bishop had been executed, the Regional Security System and the Barbados Defence Force had already started contemplating military action. In the United States, from 12 October, preparations had been made to evacuate the US nationals – mainly students – in Grenada. However, the events of Bloody Wednesday changed the dynamics. A sense of utter shock and disbelief pervaded the Caribbean. Whether supportive of his regime or not, Bishop was recognised as the Prime Minister of Grenada. His murder was unacceptable as was the accompanying civilian massacre. This led to regional calls for action and intervention.

The Prime Minister of St Lucia, John Crompton, was the first to react. In his call to Prime Minister of Tom Adams of Barbados on 20 October, he proposed multilateral intervention to restore law and order with the Caribbean nations agreeing whether or not to solicit assistance from an external power. The Barbadian Cabinet was to endorse this approach in principle while Crompton began to seek to arrange a meeting of Caribbean heads of government through the OECS and the much larger organisation of CARICOM. Reaching a consensus would be problematic.[1]

While the OECS was a small group with seven islands – Antigua and Barbuda, Dominica, St. Kitts-Nevis, St. Lucia, Montserrat, St. Vincent and Grenada. Barbados and Jamaica did not belong to the OECS but maintained close ties to the countries of that group. CARICOM was larger and included the steadfastly neutral and non-aligned country of Trinidad and Tobago and the Cooperative Republic of Guyana, which had for decades been very supportive of the Grenada Revolution and could probably be counted on to veto any military action with the support of other CARICOM members who were very wary of such an extreme option.

Adams, ever the pragmatist, understood that CARICOM would be a dead end for military intervention and as such he, alongside his similarly-minded Jamaican counterpart – Edward Seaga – realised that they had to work through the OECS, with the only problem being that neither country was a member of the OECS. To this end, one day before the CARICOM meeting arranged for 22 October, the OECS agreed to meet in Barbados and this set the foundation for either direct military action or a request to an external power – either the United Kingdom or the United States – for military intervention in Grenada.[2]

Prime Minister Adams fully appreciated that military action would be easier to justify in both the United States and the United Kingdom if a formal request came from a recognised international organisation – such as the OECS – or preferably even from Grenada itself. Adams planned to get the OECS to agree to intervene, then invite assistance from Barbados and Jamaica. Barbados would then be deputed to seek additional assistance from the United States and the United Kingdom. It was an ingenious and well-conceived plan and Adams was able to succeed without too much difficulty as he correctly gauged the OECS's mood.

The circumvention of CARICOM proved relatively easy. While Compton and the then Trinidadian Prime Minister, and chairman of CARICOM, George Chambers, tried to put together a CARICOM summit in Trinidad, Adams had already met with the US Ambassador in Barbados, Milan Bish, to urge US intervention to restore a democratic government to Grenada. Bish, who had anticipated this approach and alerted the State Department to the same, emphasised that US intervention would depend on unequivocal requests from Caribbean nations for such action. An operation to evacuate US nationals was one thing; a military intervention to effect regime change was another.

As the OECS ministers assembled at Dover Convention Centre, Adams informed the Trinidadian High Commissioner that he could not attend the CARICOM meeting because a military solution was being considered.

Tom Adams, PM of Barbados (right), Rudyard Lewis of the BDF (left), and Sir Paul Scoon. (US National Archives)

Adams then briefed the UK High Commissioner and informed him that the UK would be asked to participate, and then did the same with the US Ambassador who agreed to convey the message to President Reagan while stressing the need for a formal request. The Canadian High Commissioner was also briefed but Canadian participation was never sought nor even contemplated, despite concerns for the safety of Canadian nationals in Grenada.

The OECS, on the other hand, agreed to invoke Article 8 of their Treaty of Association which dealt with Defence and Security. The text of their decision was to state:

> The Authority proposes therefore to take action for collective defence and preservation of peace and security against external aggression by requesting assistance from friendly countries to provide transport, logistic support, and additional military personnel to assist the efforts of the OECS to stabilize this most grave situation within the Eastern Caribbean.[3]

Adams's plan had succeeded brilliantly. He had persuaded the OECS to follow a course of action to facilitate intervention and they had willingly obliged.

He later was later called to the meeting to be given an invitation to join the operation, which he accepted. Prime Minister Seaga of Jamaica was also contacted and duly accepted. Prime Minister Eugenia Charles of Dominica, along with Adams and Seaga, presented the OECS decision to Ambassador Bish on 21 October 1983. That very night, as will be shown, the Chairman of the Joint Chiefs of Staff Committee instructed Atlantic Command to include plans to militarily neutralise Grenada's PRA as well as secure the safety of American and other foreign nationals currently in Grenada.[4]

The Americans Start Planning

The United States government under Ronald Reagan was not only avowedly anti-communist but aggressively so. Earlier in 1983, President Reagan had made several references to Cuban involvement in Grenada and sparked an invasion scare when he alluded to Cuba's construction of the airport at Point Salines. His outspoken criticism against Cuba, communism and its influence in Grenada was well-established but even he balked at going into Grenada for regime change when it was entirely unclear whether the United States would have any regional support for such an operation, given the sensibilities of most countries to external intervention.

However, as will be seen later, the United States began contingency planning after Bishop's removal on 13 October. These focused on the idea that American and other foreign nationals would need to be evacuated from Grenada, possibly in a very hostile environment. It was also possible that they might become hostages against American intervention and as such plans had to be made for that contingency. The United States also contemplated a possible rescue operation for Bishop. However, between 14 and 19 October, the US had contemplated nothing more than a non-combat evacuation of foreign nationals. Bloody Wednesday, however, changed those dynamics.

The killing of Bishop, the massacre of civilians and the evident danger in Grenada immediately shifted focus. The first shift was the need to cater for an evacuation in a non-permissive environment, naturally requiring US combat troops. However, now, the United States had to consider a much more robust operation where the PRA would need to be, at the very least, kept at bay, if not destroyed, to permit such an evacuation of nationals to proceed easily. On October 20, the JCS and Atlantic Command had produced six different options with available forces, assuming no external intervention from Cuba.[5]

However, the United States was loath to escalate this operation into a full-fledged regime change affair, overthrowing the junta now running Grenada and installing a new government. For this to take place, there needed to be a formal request from a recognised international organisation of regional countries. To this end, the machinations of Adams and the OECS provided the Americans with the necessary legal foundation needed to switch the preparations from a rescue operation to a military intervention aimed at creating the environment needed for a democratic government. The OECS, Jamaica and Barbados provided this in writing by 23 October, and verbally two days earlier.[6] Once this was received, preparations for Urgent Fury moved into high gear.

Nonetheless, there was one outstanding issue – would Grenadians welcome such an intervention? No country in the Caribbean had, at that point, recognised the junta as a legitimate entity in Grenada. For a regime change intervention to have even a veneer of legitimacy, there would need to be some entity in Grenada that welcomed such an intervention. This posed a dilemma for the United States as with Bishop's death, there was no head of a recognised government. However, there was a legitimate Head of State.

The Role of Sir Paul Scoon

Sir Paul Scoon was the Governor General of Grenada. Despite its Marxist-Leninist pretentions, the Grenadian Revolutionaries never sought to replace this last vestige of colonial rule with either an Executive President or establish a Constitutional Republic with a ceremonial President as Head of State. While he had no powers of a practical nature, thanks in part to the erratic nature of the PRG's legal and constitutional systems, Sir Paul Scoon was still the last remaining constitutional authority on the island. The question remained as to whether he could be persuaded to request foreign military intervention.

On Saturday 22 October, Ken Kurze and Linda Flohr from the US embassy in Barbados, accompanied by David Montgomery, the deputy British High Commissioner to Barbados, took a charter flight to Pearls Airport in Grenada. Flohr, who was in reality a CIA case officer operating covertly, simultaneously sought to gather as much information as possible on the RMC's military capabilities and dispositions, including its anti-aircraft defences and deployments and to pass on this information to a CIA yacht using a hand-held radio. However, publicly, their immediate task was to determine how many of their nationals wished to leave Grenada and to determine the best way to evacuate them. They were tasked with discussing these issues with the officials of the RMC. There were estimated to be over 600 Americans, mainly students, and some 30 to 40 British nationals. The RMC pledged that the students and tourists were safe.[7]

Despite these reassurances, and no indication that foreign nationals were ever in any danger, the issue of evacuation got bogged down in details with the small airport at Pearls being incapable of taking anything more than small aircraft. A suggestion that a US warship could evacuate the foreigners was rejected but a proposal for a cruise liner to be pressed into service as an evacuation vessel was more favourably received as an alternative. However, while all of this was happening, David Montgomery was given a much more important and ultimately decisive task; visiting and, if necessary, persuading Sir Paul Scoon.[8]

Sir Paul Scoon, in the peculiar circumstances of a Marxist-Leninist state still having the Queen of England as its Head of State, was now,

Sir Paul Scoon. (US National Archives)

as Her Majesty's representative in that capacity, together with the powers that came therewith, the only constitutional authority on the island. While Britain was adamant against military intervention, owing to its own colonial history and involvement in the region. It was willing to send a warship to aid in evacuation but was unwilling to go further. It urged negotiations rather than military action to resolve the situation as amicably as was now practically possible.[9]

However, this was at odds with what Adams, the OECS and the Americans wanted. David Montgomery's visit to the Governor General provided an opportunity to swing things towards the desired outcome. With Sir Paul now being the sole link to any sort of legality left in Grenada, the discussions between Montgomery and Sir Paul were of vital importance. It was during this meeting that Adams was later to allege that Sir Paul Scoon verbally requested external military intervention.[10] Whether there was a verbal consent at this point in time is now, of course, moot, but there is an interesting twist in this saga which has created a degree of uncertainty as to when Sir Paul gave his consent prior to Operation Urgent Fury. Sir Paul certainly conveyed his entirely understandable concerns over the threat to his own safety, had he challenged the RMC publicly.

While this apparent verbal consent was useful, the United States required such consent for intervention to be in writing. The US State Department duly drafted an appropriately worded letter of the type that would meet with its approval and it was sent to Barbados. It was, importantly, left unsigned and undated.

Once Operation Urgent Furry got underway, copies of this letter were carried by Brigadier Rudyard Lewis of the Barbados Defence Force, Colonel Ken Barnes of the Jamaica Defence Force, CO of the Caribbean Peacekeeping Force (CPKF) and the commander of the Jamaican rifle company of the CPKF. These letters landed in Grenada on 25 October with the Caribbean troops but it was not until 26 October that Lewis was able to give his copy to Sir Paul Scoon to sign when he was safely in the care of Caribbean troops at Point Salines. This letter was, at that point in time, backdated on 24 October 1983.[11]

It is in this backdating of the letter that the confusion arises. Communication with Sir Paul prior to the start of Urgent Fury was effectively blocked. He was isolated in Government House with no means of broadcasting any message, sending any letter to foreign powers or in any way expressing his desire for external military intervention. It is known that the letter was drafted by the State Department and sent to Barbados on 23 October. It is also beyond dispute that several unsigned and undated copies landed in Grenada with Caribbean troops on October 25. Finally, it is undisputed that the letter was signed on 26 October by Sir Paul but dated 24 October 1983. The question is whether or not there was a verbal request for intervention before this written request. For this, we only have a statement from Tom Adams who, while addressing Barbadians after the end of combat operations in Urgent Fury, said:

> Now that Sir Paul Scoon is safe, I can reveal that by the kind offices of a friendly government, albeit a nonparticipating government, his views were sought well before the military operations commenced, on the issuing of an invitation to friendly countries to enter Grenada and restore order. According to my information, Sir Paul agreed to do so as soon as possible.[12]

Tom Adams watches troops of the BDF preparing to deploy to Grenada. (US National Archives)

The chronology of events was further muddied by the statements by then British Secretary of State for Foreign and Commonwealth Affairs, in which he stated, inter alia:

> Early on the 24th October, the Deputy High Commissioner in Bridgetown reported, following his brief visit to Grenada, that the Governor General (as the latter has subsequently confirmed) had made no request for Britain to intervene in Grenada.

Sir Paul himself did little to clarify things when interviewed by the BBC in the aftermath of the intervention. Sir Paul stated that he had not considered intervention necessary until late on Sunday evening – 23

October 1983 – after David Montgomery would have left. Had he made any such verbal request, it is probable that it would have found prominent mention in the report of Montgomery. Even President Reagan made no mention of such a request when he spoke to Prime Minister Thatcher on 23 October. It is hard to escape the conclusion that, whatever his own views, the first that Sir Paul Scoon knew of his appeal for foreign military intervention was when Brigadier Lewis asked him to sign the letter requesting such military intervention on 26 October at Point Salines.[13] At this point, he could hardly refuse.

It is therefore quite likely that the decision to intervene and oust the junta in Grenada was made on the basis of it being an opportunity too good to allow to escape. It was justified by a possible danger to US citizens (one that was real, if unlikely) and an urgent plea for assistance from the states of the OECS as well as Barbados and Jamaica. Sir Paul's alleged verbal request was in all likelihood a post-fact invention aimed at strengthening the legal basis for such an intervention. Yet, Sir Paul could not be happy with the situation in Grenada.

In hindsight, consideration should be given to his stated view that by late evening on 23 October, he considered intervention necessary. His own memoirs put things in a most backhanded manner:

> ... if a military operation to achieve [law and order] were to be undertaken by our sister states – if necessary, with assistance of the United States, I would give such an initiative my fullest support.[14]

Countdown to War

While all these shenanigans were going on, CARICOM leaders met on Saturday 22 October. Grenada was expelled from CARICOM and sanctions imposed over the objections of Guyana. As expected, Trinidad, Belize, Bahamas and Guyana opposed military intervention. However, it was now evident that the OECS had plans of its own. President Forbes Burnham of Guyana telephoned Havana before his departure to warn of OECS plans. By that evening, Radio Free Grenada announced that an invasion was now imminent.

4
OPPOSING FORCES

The United States and its Allies

An underappreciated aspect of Operation Urgent Fury is the fact that the United States strove to establish a multi-national alliance of countries unhappy with the developments in Grenada and seeking a restoration of some form of democratic order. To this end, though the United States armed forces did all of the fighting during Operation Urgent Fury, and took all the casualties, in the aftermath, the United States had the able assistance of the Barbados and Jamaica Defence Forces and the Caribbean Peacekeeping Force with its useful mixture of military and police personnel. The role of the Regional Security System is underappreciated and its part in the events of October 1983 must be acknowledged.

While many books have covered the United States forces in excruciating detail, the other forces have remained largely under-acknowledged but they have rich histories and evolutions which will be detailed in the text. Barbados, in particular, was to play an outsized role in the prelude to Operation Urgent Fury, conducting reconnaissance and intelligence operations far outweighing its military role. These will be detailed in the following chapter. Jamaica, on the other hand, ably led the Caribbean peacekeepers in the chaotic aftermath.

Vice Admiral Joseph Metcalf III, overall commander of Operation Urgent Fury. (Albert Grandolini Collection)

United States Forces

When the scale of the unrest in Grenada became evident, the United States began planning for an evacuation of its nationals from the island. The US Joint Staff's crisis response team was ordered to work with Atlantic Command to prepare a range of evacuation options – ranging from a peaceful, uncontested evacuation, to one which involved the use of force. As the events in Grenada escalated, on 18 October 1983, Atlantic Command activated its own crisis action team and began to prepare for the possibility that military force might be needed for deployment to Grenada at short notice.[1] Overall command was vested in Vice Admiral Joseph Metcalf III with Major General H. Norman Schwarzkopf as his land forces advisor.

The United States laboured under an extreme dearth of reliable information. This produced wildly inflated figures for the potential adversaries. US estimates put the regular PRA at some 1,200 personnel with the PRA being able to field an additional 3,000. The Cuban construction workers were viewed as combatants with the potential to field over 700 trained soldiers, thus giving an American estimate of a potential opposition that numbered close to 5,000 personnel under arms and prepared to fight any intervention force that sought to evacuate American nationals. This was an absolute nonsense. The PRAF, as will be seen, was able to muster under 800 troops and the Cubans were not prepared to fully participate in the defence of the RMC.

USS *Guam* (LPH-9) in late 1983. This Iwo Jima-class amphibious assault ship had a crew of 718 and could embark up to 25 helicopters. *Guam* was commissioned to service with the US Navy in January 1965, and saw extensive service in the Atlantic, Mediterranean and Caribbean during the 1970s. (US DoD)

USS *Guam* (LPH-9), in August 1990, by when the Basic Point Defence Missile System and the Mk.15 Phalanx close-in weapons system had been installed. (US DoD)

A USMC AH-1T Sea Cobra during Operation Urgent Fury, firing its 20mm cannon over the sea. (US DoD)

Nonetheless, given the savagery of the events of 19 October 1983, the United States could not afford to be complacent. With over 700 US students on the island – plus many nationals from friendly foreign countries such as Canada and the United Kingdom – planning had to cater for a potential worst-case scenario, with the students and even the Governor General being held hostage to ward off intervention.

To this end, the United States prepared an overwhelming force. Over 60 combat aircraft aboard the USS *Independence* (F-14 fighters, A-6 bombers and A-7 attack aircraft), Spectre gunships of the 16th Special Operations squadron, plus well over 100 helicopters – comprising those of the Marine Medium Helicopter Squadron 261, augmented by detachments from Marine Heavy Helicopter Squadron 362 and Marine Light Attack Helicopter Squadron 167; plus those of Task Force 160 supporting the Special Operations Forces of Joint Task Force 123 and the attached Combat Aviation Battalion attached to the 82nd Airborne Division – formed a formidable array of air power. These were ably supported by transport aircraft – C-130s and C-141s of the Military Airlift Command – inflight refuelling tankers, E-3 Sentry Airborne Early Warning aircraft and F-15 fighters from the United States

US 60mm mortar crew of the USMC during a break in the action in Grenada. (US National Archives)

Air Force, the two types being deployed to Puerto Rico for air defence duties and to monitor the Cuban Air Force.

This airpower overkill might seem excessive given the fact that Grenada had no transport aircraft, much less combat aircraft, no surface-to-air missiles and not even a radar to detect incoming aircraft. However, Cold War paranoia and a lack of information regarding Cuban intentions meant that intervention by the powerful Cuban Air Force could not be discounted.

For ground operations, the United States brought to bear all available weapons normally held by Marine Amphibious Units and the 82nd Airborne Division. The Marines brought with them armour in the form of M60A1 battle tanks while their artillery comprised 155mm towed howitzers. The 82nd Airborne brought with it no armour but was well equipped for deployment with jeep-mounted TOW anti-tank missiles and lighter artillery in the form of towed 105mm howitzers.

Navy and Marine Units

The US Navy's Amphibious Squadron Four embarked the men and equipment of the 22nd Marine Amphibious Unit at Morehead City, North Carolina. Initially intended for deployment to Lebanon, the 22nd MAU was diverted for possible deployment to Grenada. Its commander was Captain (N) Carl R. Erie, an experienced aviator. The ships at his disposal included the amphibious assault ship, the USS *Guam*, which served as flagship; the amphibious transport dock, the USS *Trenton*; the dock landing ship, USS *Fort Snelling*; and, lastly, two landing ships, the USS *Manitowoc* and the USS *Barnstable County*.[2] While Amphibious Squadron Four was in the Atlantic en route to Lebanon, the events of 19 October 1983, prompted an immediate turnabout of this force which headed to the Caribbean island.

The 22nd MAU was a combined air and ground task force, the Marine Amphibious Units being the smallest of such combined

One of five M60A1 tanks of the 22nd MAU deployed in St George's. (US National Archives)

A pair of LTVP-7s deployed on Carriacou Island, Grenada: the 22nd MAU made use of 13 such amphibious vehicles during Operation Urgent Fury. (US National Archives)

A USMC CH-46 Sea Knight of the 22nd MAU. (US National Archives)

of the PRA, being available to the infantry units. In addition, the integral support weapons company had 10 Dragon man-portable ATGMs and a mortar platoon with 81mm mortars was available for fire support.[4] A number of jeeps armed with M60 machine guns were also available for both transport and for reconnaissance operations.

In addition, the 22nd MAU brought with them integral armoured units with LVTP-7 amphibian assault personnel carriers and, much more importantly, the M60A1 tanks of the 3rd Platoon of A Company of the 2nd Tank Battalion. Of note, when deployed in Grenada, these tanks left the 105mm ammunition for their main guns aboard the ships of Task Force 124. In addition, H Battery of the 3/10 Artillery battalion with 155mm towed howitzers was attached to the 22nd MAU but some troops of this battery ended up being deployed as infantry during Operation Urgent Fury, their artillery being unnecessary to the task at hand.[5]

Other naval support was to be found in the form of Carrier Battle Group 10 which was centred around the aircraft carrier USS *Independence* escorted by two guided-missile destroyers the USS *Richmond K. Turner* (CO-20) and the USS *Coontz* (DDG-40); two destroyers, USS *Caron* (DD-970) and USS *Moosbrugger* (DD-980); one guided-missile frigate, the USS *Clifton Sprague* (FFG-16) and the ammunition ship USS *Suribachi* (AE-21).[6] This force was redesignated as Task Group 20-5 and was also diverted from its original course to Lebanon, escorting Amphibious Squadron Four.

The USS *Independence* brought with it some 90 combat aircraft of Carrier Air Wing 6. This air wing had the following squadrons; Fighter Squadron 32 (VF-32); Fighter Squadron 14 (VF-14); Attack Squadron 176 (VA-176); Attack Squadron 87 (VA-87); Attack Squadron 15 (VA-15); Airborne Early Warning Squadron 122 (VAW-122); Tactical Electronic Warfare Squadron 131 (VAQ-131); Helicopter Anti-submarine Squadron 15 (HS-15) and Air Anti-submarine Squadron 28 (VS-28). The two fighter squadrons were equipped with F-14 Tomcats; VA-176 was equipped with A-6E Intruder bombers; VA-87 and VA-15 were equipped with A-7E Corsair-II fighter bombers while E-2Cs, EA-6Bs, SH-3 helicopters

Marine units. The 22nd MAU was commanded by Marine Colonel James P. Faulkner, and consisted of a small headquarters element, a battalion landing team (the 2nd Battalion, 8th Marines), a helicopter squadron – with heavy (CH-53) and medium (CH-46) transport helicopters and AH-1 Cobra helicopter gunships – and a support group with maintenance, support and service units.[3] The 22nd MAU had about 1,900 men, a force that proved to be significantly larger than the combined total of hostile forces that the US forces ended up facing on Grenada – inclusive of Cubans and Grenadians. Amphibious Squadron Four was to become Task Force 124, with the 22nd MAU being designated Task Group 124.2. Of great advantage to the US Navy and Marines was the self-contained nature of their combat formations with 60mm mortars and machine guns and anti-tank weapons in the form of 66mm LAW rockets and 90mm recoilless rifles, the latter being devastating against the BTR-60s

A USMC CH-53D Sea Stallion helicopter on the deck of USS *Guam*, with Marines embarking. (US DoD)

USS *Independence* (CV-62; background) during underway replenishment from USS *Canisteo* (AO-99; centre), in company of the guided missile destroyer USS *Luce* (DDG-38) in 1981. (US National Archives)

and S-3 Vikings rounded out the rest of the air wing.[7] In total, Carrier Air Wing 6 had some 60 combat aircraft at its disposal, the three attack squadrons proving to be invaluable during Operation Urgent Fury.

Special Operations Forces

Operating under Atlantic Command, the Special Operations Forces earmarked for Urgent Fury were grouped into Joint Task Force 123. The Special Operations Force consisted of two detachments of Navy SEALs – Teams A and B – and a team from the US Army's Delta Force. They were supported by two companies from the 75th Ranger Battalion (1/75 and 2/75) with aviation support provided by the AC-130H 'Spectre' gunships of the 16th Special Operations Squadron and the helicopters of TF 160 – MH-6 'Little Bird' for attack and UH-60 'Blackhawks' for transport.[8] The Special Operations Forces of JTF 123 were the spearhead of Operation Urgent Fury and took heavy casualties in the initial hours of the assault. It should be noted that unlike follow-on Army units, and the Marines of 22nd MAU, the Special Forces did not have either any armour or support weapons and could have been possibly overwhelmed had the PRA been in a position to mass its concentrated mobile and motorised forces against them in the initial stages of the operation.

82nd Airborne Division

The 82nd Airborne Division contributed elements of two brigades – 2nd and 3rd – to Operation Urgent Fury. These were augmented by

UH-60A Black Hawk helicopters of TF 160. (US DoD)

A UH-60A of TF 160 on the deck of USS *Guam* during Operation Urgent Fury. (US DoD)

An M101 105mm howitzer of 82nd Airborne Division with its crew and ammunition. (US DoD)

a Combat Aviation Battalion. The 2nd Brigade deployed elements of two airborne infantry battalions – 325th and 508th – with artillery support. Each infantry battalion had three rifle companies and an anti-tank company. The rifle companies had 60mm mortars and Dragon anti-tank missiles for support. The anti-tank company had jeep-mounted TOW anti-tank missiles. The two artillery batteries – one of which was at reduced strength – had towed 105mm howitzers.[9] The 3rd Brigade of the 82nd Airborne fielded elements of the 505th and 508th airborne infantry battalions

An M151 MUTT jeep of the 82nd Airborne Division, with BGM-71 TOW anti-tank guided missile system, in St. George's. (US National Archives)

Troops of the 82nd Airborne Division, two of them carrying M47 Dragon anti-tank guided missiles, inspecting a home in Grenada during Operation Urgent Fury. (US National Archives)

with three artillery batteries also equipped with 105mm howitzers. Both brigades had a company-sized unit of Military Police and an air defence platoon with Stinger man-portable SAMs. Together, the two brigades of the 82nd Airborne probably contributed the single largest combat formation to Operation Fury but did not participate in the initial assault – that being confined to the Special Operations Force and the 22nd MAU. Crucial to their success, however, was the Combat Aviation Battalion with its UH-60 'Blackhawk' helicopters.

Deployed US Ground Forces

In the aftermath and facing some criticism for the 'excessive' force alleged to have been used by the United States – some based on incorrect information as will be detailed in the next chapter – there were a number of considerations that the United States had to take into account. Writing in *Military Review*, Captain D.P. Bolger noted:

The total possible opposition to the US operation was 10 battalions plus combat support and combat service support units. US staff planning officers had to plan for the worst case. As it turned out, both the Cubans (who had almost 12 percent casualties) and the Grenadian PRA fought hard for the first two days. The PRM did not contribute much to the island's defense.

Terrain and weather also influenced US force levels. Grenada is not a small, flat, desert island. Its area is 119 square miles (311 square kilometers). Grenada's volcanic, hilly terrain is heavily vegetated. Its population of about 110,000 occupies the land at a greater density than is found in Massachusetts or Connecticut. In the Caribbean, only Puerto Rico has more people per square mile. Almost 30,000 Grenadians live in and around St. George's. The rest are spread in small towns and clusters of farm huts. About 12 percent of the island is primary rain forest, with most of the rest either secondary forest or cultivated cocoa, banana and nutmeg groves. The central rock formations and heavy vegetation limit areas for helicopter landing zones. The hot, humid air averages 82 degrees Fahrenheit which would affect US troops. The only real coastal plain is in the Point Salines area, and most beaches are treacherous, even for small boats, let alone landing craft.

Two factors influenced force planners. The large population required precision in ground operations. Foot reconnaissance would have to be used in lieu of reconnaissance by fire. Also, the defenders had many camouflage advantages. The precipitous topography would absorb a lot of infantry. Securing Grenada with vehicles or helicopter scouts would not be very effective. Too much could transpire unseen under the trees.

Troops available for the operation were limited by time constraints and mission requirements. The Caribbean area comes under the US Atlantic Command; the USS *Independence* and Navy/Marine amphibious group were already available. Special Operations Forces were selected for a few critical tasks.

> US Atlantic Command planners could reinforce the MAU by sea or by air. Sea transport takes a long time, and the dispatch of additional MAUs was ruled out. Air reinforcement was quicker but required the seizure of one or more runways. Army paratroopers were the logical choice, and the Army Rangers had trained to rescue hostages. Thus, the airborne Ranger battalions were added. More infantrymen were needed to complete the clearance of the countryside, and the 82d Airborne Division was the closest source of nonmechanized troops. They also had the ability to parachute into Grenada if necessary, and their normal readiness level is higher than other available Army units.
>
> Force planners allocated the two Ranger battalions with Air Force airlift, the MAU, Air Force *Spectre* gunships and the USS *Independence* attack aircraft to the assault echelon. Air Force Military Airlift Command (MAC) planes would deliver the Caribbean peacekeeping force and two brigades of the 82nd Airborne Division for reinforcements. The actual force ratios during the campaign proved adequate. However, the pace of US reinforcement indicates that the assault elements fought and won the major engagements without any overwhelming superiority in numbers or excessive use of firepower. US troop strength peaked as the Rangers were withdrawn. The redeployment schedule was dependent on the MAC airflow. The 82nd Airborne Division was not flown in to meet unexpectedly heavy resistance.[10]

Moreover, as would be expected, any military operation aims at crushing its opposition through the use of superior force wherever possible. While a legitimate criticism of the United States deployment was its completely inflated opinion of the force levels it would face, it is also to be noted that the US was unable to deploy its entire designated force simultaneously. Troops were inducted in a phased manner and were limited in number.

In theory, the United States thought it would be facing the equivalent of 10 battalions of infantry, with armour, artillery and anti-aircraft weapons. This of course was completely nonsensical but planners in the United States had to cater for every contingency. It was better that the opposition was overestimated rather than underestimated. Force levels were also dictated by the mission priorities and American strategic objectives:

> The US military missions in Grenada were established from the President's strategic objectives. The safety of the medical students, not the destruction of the Cuban/PRA forces, was the immediate objective. As a result, US forces were initially directed against those opposition forces posing the greatest threat to the US citizens on the island. The civilian presence discouraged the massive use of mortar, artillery or naval gunfire, and air munitions.
>
> The second objective was the restoration of a democratic government. This necessitated the destruction of the PRA. There had to be an island left to restore, so collateral damage and civilian casualties had to be held to a minimum. Equally important, there had to be enough US troops on the ground to physically sweep and control the island to prevent any Cuban/PRA guerrilla campaign. The elimination of the Cuban presence – the third objective – implied the isolation, destruction, or capture and removal of the Cubans.
>
> In essence, rescue operations had priority. The US rules of engagement required minimum force and minimum casualties. With these constraints, the force structure had to include enough troop strength to handle the likely opposition without resorting to massive firepower.[11]

The United States, anticipating a substantial hostile force, committed to an operation that would inevitably somewhat preclude the use of overwhelming firepower, thus built its force levels to a degree to which they could feel comfortable in completing their assigned mission without trouble.

The US forces were thus very well equipped to confront any likely opposition in Grenada. However, they were completely ignorant of the island and, as the regional superpower, they were viewed with extreme suspicion by many within the Caribbean. To this end, the United States actively sought assistance from regional partners, firstly through the Organisation of Eastern Caribbean States (OECS) and the Regional Security System, but also directly through its contacts in Jamaica and Barbados. The defence forces of these two countries were to play an important role, albeit post-combat, as peacekeepers, in Grenada and are worth studying in some detail.

The Barbados Defence Force – 1980s capabilities

The BDF was formed, at least in part, out of the regional political situation which saw, in October 1976, two separate incidents. One involved the bizarre incident of a Barbadian national, resident overseas, by the name of Sidney Burnett-Alleyne, who was intercepted off the coast of Martinique, apparently planning to overthrow the Barbadian government. The second incident, on 6 October, saw the destruction of a Cubana airliner after its departure from the international airport in Barbados. Three years later, the revolution in Grenada, which ousted the despotic Prime Minister Eric Gairy in favour of the Marxist New JEWEL government of Maurice Bishop, posed an apparent threat to democratic states in the region.[12] Although there was no immediate threat of communist insurrection in any of the other countries of the English-speaking Caribbean, the spectre of Bishop's success, his charisma and the appeal of his revolutionary rhetoric gave cause for concern among the more staid, conservative, Afro-Saxon leaders of the region, especially given Cuba's open support for the Grenadian revolution and the rapid build-up and expansion of that country's armed forces.

This reinforced the view of the Barbadian leadership, then under the Barbados Labour Party led by Tom Adams, that the creation of the BDF was the correct step and was needed to provide improved security for the island. This became ever more necessary since Sidney Burnett-Alleyne made no secret of his intention to continue to try to overthrow the government of Barbados and declare himself archduke of the country![13] Burnett-Alleyne's threats, as comical as they might seem, were to be taken seriously as he was a known arms smuggler and was able to interact with mercenaries. To that extent, Burnett-Alleyne was deemed to pose a real danger to an island like Barbados, which, during his initial coup-plotting attempts, did not have a military of any significance with which to oppose an armed attempt to oust a government. Grenada proved that a small force of insurgents, with a reasonable level of organisation, could overthrow a government, despite the latter having an armed police force at its disposal, without undue difficulty.

The BDF – Formation and Policy Orientation

The BDF, small as it was with only a sub-strength infantry battalion with five sub-units, was soon being used in action as an element of Barbadian foreign policy. The BDF initially included an administrative 'squadron', an infantry element, also then termed a 'squadron', the Barbados Regiment (for ceremonial purposes), a pioneer (or engineering purposes) squadron and the Barbados Coast Guard.[14] The force was small, not particularly well-equipped – using a mixture of vintage weapons and more up-to-date NATO standard rifles and machine guns – and had limited transport resources and next to no useable air support, being dependent on civilian aircraft. Its deployment on overseas operations, therefore, was more for prestige than practical effect.

The Formation of the Barbados Coast Guard

As indicated earlier, the Barbados Coast Guard Service was established as a civilian unit in August 1974 and initially located at Enterprise, Christ Church. As a civilian service, the roles of the Coast Guard Service in this civilian period were limited to search and rescue, investigating the illegal entry of persons and goods, while enforcing the law against the dynamiting of fish around the coastal waters of Barbados.

This civilian service, known as the Coast Guard Civilian Unit Service, served for over four years but was finally dissolved in September 1978. With the decision being taken to create a Barbados Defence Force, the Coast Guard was briefly known as the Maritime Wing of the Barbados Regiment. However, the Defence Act of 1979 (Part X) created the legislative framework needed for the creation of the Barbados Coast Guard to serve as the maritime element of the new Barbados Defence Force. Under the Defence Act, the Coast Guard now had expanded roles and responsibilities and is now formally an armed service, subject to military discipline and rules. The shift from a civilian agency to a militarised entity has allowed for improved equipment and armed vessels.[15]

By the 1980s, the Barbados Coast Guard had some 125 personnel, a strength it maintained into the mid-1990s. Its largest asset, until it was decommissioned and scuttled in 2016, was the *Trident,* a 37.5m British-built patrol boat that entered service in 1981. This vessel, equipped with a 40mm gun (later replaced by a 20mm weapon), was the largest vessel in the Barbados Coast Guard, supplemented by six other vessels. These included one 30-ton *Guardian* class vessel (out of a total of three acquired in the 1970s), a 11.5-ton Lewis-class vessel – both being British-built – and two converted shrimp boats.[16]

The Barbados Defence Force Air Wing

Barbados established a security air wing in 1971 but shortly after its formation in 1979, the BDF created an Air Wing which first operated a leased Beech Queen Air. In 1981, after the lease of the aircraft expired, the BDF obtained, and owned, a single Cessna 402. Surprisingly, this aircraft was retired in 1985 and has not been replaced to date.[17]

THE JAMAICA DEFENCE FORCE IN THE 1980s

The Jamaica Regiment

In the aftermath of the disbanding of the West Indies Regiment and the collapse of the Federation, the First Battalion and Third Battalion of the latter became the First Battalion and Third Battalion of the Jamaica Regiment respectively. The Second Battalion was to become the nucleus of the Trinidad and Tobago Regiment. In the prelude to independence, the Jamaica Local Forces (JLF) were formed as one of the conditions under which Jamaica was granted independence. The JLF was to eventually become the Jamaica Defence Force and its component land, sea and air elements, the latter two being very modest to start, were tasked with the following duties:

- Defence against military or paramilitary threats
- Military aid to Civil Authorities
- Internal Security Support
- Counter-narcotics Operations
- Search and Rescue (SAR) Operations
- Humanitarian and disaster relief
- Counter Terrorism
- State ceremonials[18]

For decades, the Jamaica Regiment had two Regular Infantry Battalions – the 1st Battalion the Jamaica Regiment and the 2nd Battalion the Jamaica Regiment – which rotated their deployment between the Lathbury Barracks, located at Up Park Camp, Kingston and the Moneague Training Camp, Moneague, St Ann. This rotation is usually done at the beginning of each year and allows for familiarisation of each unit.[19]

Both battalions were tasked with assisting the Jamaica Constabulary Force (JCF) in maintaining law and order in designated areas which are deemed to warrant military deployment. To this end, a Joint Task Force Headquarters comprising command elements from both the JCF and the JDF has been established and functions to date.

The senior unit of the Jamaica Regiment is the First Battalion, The Jamaica Regiment (1JR) and was formed on the 31 July 1962. It was formed with an initial strength of four rifle companies, a support company and a headquarters company. However, by 1979, the battalion had grown to eight companies and was becoming administratively unwieldy.[20]

By the late 1970s there was an acceptance that a second regular infantry battalion was needed. The 1970s saw a good deal of electoral violence in Jamaica and the JDF was heavily committed to supporting the JCF in trying to keep political violence to within manageable levels. In May the battalion was split in two.

A Cessna 402C of the Barbados Defence Force. (BDF)

Four companies remained as the First Battalion, Jamaica Regiment while the other four companies were used to form the Second Battalion, Jamaica Regiment, whose home base became the Moneague Training Camp in St. Ann. Thus, on 21 May 1979, the Second Battalion, the Jamaica Regiment (2JR) mustered for the first time in the Men's Dining Hall at the Moneague Training Camp in St. Ann and

Jamaica Regiment V-150 APCs in Kingston. (JDF)

was in action within a few weeks in disaster relief operations during heavy flooding in 1979.[21]

The Jamaica Regiment's reserve formation was, until recently, the Third Battalion of the Jamaica Regiment. Formally designated as the Third Battalion, Jamaica Regiment (National Reserve), the personnel of the unit, after undergoing initial training, are only required to serve a minimum of 19 days in each year, thus allowing people with regular employment to serve in the military. The National Reserve has four barracks across Jamaica: Curphey Barracks – Up Park Camp; Foster Barracks – Mandeville; Burke Barracks – Montego Bay; and Whitehorne Barracks – Port Maria.[22] As befitting its major encampment, Up Park Camp houses the Third Battalion's headquarters, the Headquarter Company, and two rifle companies, 'Alpha' and 'Bravo'. As might be expected for reserve formations, each of the rifle companies was headed by a Training Major while the regular force provides a cadre of senior NCOs for the National Reserve.[23]

The equipment available to the Jamaica Regiment was almost exclusively of British origin until the 1990s. The main battle rifle was the 7.62mm L1A1 SLR rifle, with the Sterling submachine gun, FN MAG general-purpose machine gun, 51mm mortars and M79 grenade launcher rounding out the infantry weapons issued at section, platoon and company level. Battalion fire support is centred around 81mm L16 mortars.

Unlike the armed forces of other islands of the English-speaking Caribbean (as against Guyana), the Jamaica Regiment invested in a force of armoured vehicles early in its history with a small number of Ferret armoured cars – perhaps as many as 15 – being available even in the early years of its formation. Unlike the two Dingo armoured cars available to the Trinidad and Tobago Regiment, Jamaica's Ferrets were fully operational vehicles, intended for internal security operations. These armoured cars were armed with machine guns but is unclear as to how long they were retained in service as they were likely to be second-hand Ferret Mk.4s and as such had been heavily used before delivery to Jamaica in the 1960s. It is likely they were withdrawn in the 1970s.

The Ferrets augmented a force of machine gun-armed trailer-trucks supplied by the United States of America but both the Ferrets and the machine gun trucks were supplemented and largely supplanted by a force of some 14 V-150 Cadillac Gage armoured personnel carriers.[24]

The Jamaican Defence Force Air Wing

The Jamaican Defence Air Wing was formed in June 1963, initially as the Jamaican Air Squadron with pilots from the civilian Jamaican Flying Club. One month later, the Jamaican Defence Force Air Wing was established on the 3 July 1963 with the arrival of four Cessna 185s. These were later joined by a small force of two Bell 47G helicopters that were ferry-flown to Jamaica from Texas.[25]

Flying training was carried out in England until 1972 and after that in Canada, but Jamaica has made strenuous efforts to develop an indigenous training capability. During the 1970s, from 1971 to 1973, the Air Wing received some Bell 206 and Bell 212 helicopters. The former type was to become a major element in the Air Wing's operational and training inventory, with a single type continuing in service to date. The Bell 212s, three of which were delivered in 1973, lasted in service until 1998 when they were withdrawn from use.[26]

Table 1: Aircraft Available to the JDF Air Wing in 1983[28]

Aircraft Type	Quantity	Service Entry	Out of Service	Origin
Aerospatiale AS 355 Ecureuil	4	1999	2007	France
Beech A100 King Air	1	1975	2003	USA
Bell 47G Sioux	2	1963	1971	USA
Bell 205A	4	1974	1975	USA
Bell 206 JetRanger	8	1971	current	USA
Bell 212 Twin Huey	3	1973	1998	USA
Britten-Norman BN-2A Islander	2	1974	2012	UK
Cessna 185 Skywagon	4	1963	1977	USA
Cessna 210 Centurion	3	1983	2011	USA
Cessna 337G (O-2A) Skymaster	1	1983	1994	USA
De Havilland Canada DHC-6 Twin Otter	1	1967	1978	Canada

In April 1977 the Air Wing became an autonomous unit within the JDF but was still largely subordinated to the Jamaica Regiment. A number of light transport and liaison aircraft were procured from the 1970s onwards with the Britten-Norman BN-2 being the most effective of these assets. However, various Cessna light aircraft were to predominate in the Air Wing, these being principally tasked with light transport duties with some limited use in the maritime patrol role, though they were never equipped with any sensors fit for the task.[27]

The Jamaica Coast Guard

The naval arm of the JDF was formed in 1963, one year after the formation of the JDF. This naval arm was called the 'Jamaica Sea Squadron' and was established with an initial complement of three 63-foot wooden Second World War torpedo recovery boats provided by the United States Government. These vessels were commissioned HMJS *Yoruba* (P1), HMJS *Coromante* (P2) and HMJS *Mandingo* (P3), where HMJS is *Her Majesty's Jamaican Ship*. As was common with the English-speaking Caribbean, a training team from the Royal Navy assisted with the Sea Squadron's early development.[29]

Some four years later, the Sea Squadron was renamed the Jamaica Defence Force Coast Guard (JDF CG) in 1966. In the tradition of British-inspired forces, a naval White Ensign, naval rank insignia and Royal Navy-pattern uniforms were adopted. It should be noted that the JDF Coast Guard nominally holds Army ranks, similar to the Air Wing and the Jamaica Regiment. This reflects the relatively subordinate role of the Coast Guard to the Jamaica Regiment and its land forces. This would seem to be counterintuitive for an island nation, but Jamaica's terrestrial internal security challenges have meant a focus on land forces.

In 1966, the JDF Coast Guard got rid of its wholly inadequate 63-foot boats and acquired the first of three 85-foot all-aluminium Bay Class Patrol Boats. These vessels, HMJS *Discovery Bay* (P4), HMJS *Holland Bay* (P5) and HMJS *Manatee Bay* (P6), were commissioned between 1966 and1967. The Bay Class vessels were modified commercial cabin cruiser designs and lasted in service well into the 1990s, though were of dubious serviceability. The HMJS *Holland Bay* (P5) lasted until 2003, with at least two refits being undertaken.[30]

In 1974, the JDF Coast Guard acquired the first of two 'offshore' patrol vessels with the HMJS *Fort Charles* (P7) being acquired. This vessel was 103 feet long and displaced 103 tons and was armed with a 20mm gun and two 0.50 calibre M2HB guns with a crew of 20. The *Fort Charles* was followed in 1985 by the HMJS *Paul Bogle* (P8) which was similarly equipped.[31] In 1983, the JDF Coast Guard was largely a coastal force with few pretentions of external deployment capability.

Regional Security Structures

CARICOM does not operate any joint military forces and the defence forces of the individual countries are resolutely separate, to the extent of having minimal equipment compatibility. However, there is one joint security entity that has stood the test of time and has performed well whenever called upon. This is the Regional Security System (RSS) which details its history and mission as follows:

> The Regional Security System (RSS) was created out of a need for a collective response to security threats, which were impacting on the stability of the region in the early 1970s and 1980s. In October 1982, four members of the Organisation of the Eastern Caribbean States, namely, Antigua & Barbuda, Dominica, St. Lucia and St. Vincent and the Grenadines, signed a Memorandum of Understanding (MOU) with Barbados to provide for 'mutual assistance on request'. St. Kitts and Nevis joined after gaining independence in September 1983 and Grenada in January 1985. The MOU was updated in 1992 and the RSS acquired juridical status in March 1996 by way of the Treaty which was signed in St. George's, Grenada.[32]

The RSS does not include either Jamaica, Guyana or Trinidad and Tobago, though all three countries have collaborated with the RSS on occasion. Jamaica, for example, contributed troops to Urgent Fury, at least partly coordinated through the RSS, and Trinidad and Tobago benefitted enormously when CARICOM troops, coordinated through the RSS, arrived to assist with law and order duties in the aftermath of the 1990 coup. Another major function of the RSS is to provide coordination in respect of disaster relief operations, this being most recently done in Dominica following the devastation of Hurricane Maria in 2017.

The First Test of the RSS[33]

The RSS played an important role in coordinating the OECS military response and seven CARICOM countries sent security personnel to assist. Jamaica sent some 150 troops, Barbados 50 and Antigua and Barbuda sent a single infantry squad. Other members Dominica, St. Lucia, St. Vincent and the Grenadines and St. Kitts and Nevis, plus Barbados, sent police or members of their police SSUs to form a Caribbean Peace Keeping Force of some 350 personnel. These would be deployed in a non-combat role.

Caribbean Peacekeeping Force

The JDF, while not part of the RSS, had an important role to play during the 1983 US intervention in Grenada. Unlike Barbados, however, the JDF had little role in the planning or reconnaissance undertaken prior to the operation and while Jamaica was supportive of the intervention, its government was not as proactive as the

Troops of the CPKF on guard duty. (US DoD)

Eastern Caribbean States or Barbados in terms of organising or encouraging intervention in Grenada. However, once it was decided that a Caribbean Peace Keeping Force was to be sent to Grenada, the Jamaica Regiment was called upon to provide leadership and troops. It was always understood that the CPKF would be entirely dependent on the United States for transporting its assets and for logistical support. In this regard, the RSS proved to be an invaluable coordinating entity and despite a multiplicity of forces involved, the CPKF was relatively easily formed and prepared for deployment.

While Brigadier Rudyard Lewis (he had been promoted from Colonel for the role) of Barbados was given the task as regional coordinator, Colonel Ken Barnes of the Jamaica Defence Force was given command of the Caribbean Peace Keeping Force. To the reinforced rifle platoon of the Barbados Defence Force and the 100 policemen of the Barbados police force and 50 assorted police personnel from other Caribbean islands, the Jamaica Regiment dispatched a full rifle company of 120 personnel, a mortar section with two 81mm mortars and a medical section for a total of 150 JDF personnel being committed to Grenada, making it the only fully contained combat element of the CPKF.[34]

While the CPKF saw no combat, it was tasked with guarding prisoners, particularly those of the Grenadian People's Revolutionary Army, and with other military police functions. The Jamaica Defence Force personnel were much appreciated by their United States military counterparts and the strong sense of military professionalism enabled the JDF contingent to perform well and extricate itself from Grenada with no blemishes upon its reputation despite the fraught internal situation following the American military intervention.[35] No major allegations of abuse were levelled at the JDF units and despite its unfamiliarity of the country, the JDF led the CPKF reasonably competently.

The People's Revolutionary Armed Forces of Grenada

The opposition to the US intervention forces was spearheaded by the People's Revolutionary Armed Forces (PRAF). This comprised of the People's Revolutionary Army (PRA) and the People's Revolutionary Militia (PRM). While the PRA had some degree of military training, was reasonably well-equipped and possessed a nucleus of qualified professional soldiers, the same could not be said of the PRM which was largely a poorly trained, indifferently equipped and militarily insignificant force largely used as a social and neighbourhood mobilisation force with emphasis being placed on loyalty to the NJM and its PRG rather than on armed roles outside of the most basic of internal security duties. It should also be noted that the RGPF, renamed as the Grenada Police Service for the duration of the NJM/PRG rule, was largely restricted to traffic control and the control of crime. It had little credibility left because of its close alliance to Gairy's regime and its armed role was reduced even further, with its stocks of weapons being kept in store. The police, therefore, played no role in opposing the US-led intervention and were later completely reorganised, revamped and retrained with the assistance of the Barbados Police Force in the aftermath of Urgent Fury, with excellent results despite a number of its initial recruits being ex-PRA/PRM personnel.

One point of importance, which cannot be over-emphasised, is that the PRAF were loyal to Bishop above the NJM or PRG. This was not out of any demagoguery or blind indoctrination. Bishop, to the end of his life, and despite the sins of commission and omission of his government, remained extremely popular within Grenada and the members of the PRAF were no exception. Their morale, after his murder, and their own role in it, was extremely low. This was particularly true of the PRM which was now largely distrusted by the new RMC and, as will be detailed, when the call to arms came from the RMC to resist the US intervention forces, only one in 10 of the militia's ostensible strength showed up for duty and even these were of dubious loyalty in respect of their commitment to the RMC. The PRA, never particularly large at the best of time, perhaps mobilised only about half its sanctioned strength but these troops, within their limitations, fought well.

Organisation and Strength of the PRAF

The growth of the PRAF was at the same time both theoretically spectacular and practically very modest. Growing out of the NJM's NLA, the PRAF was immediately seen by the new PRG government as an instrument to replace the old and discredited Gairy security apparatus. To this end, the PRA was established and by 1980, had grown considerably, although its practical capability remained minimal. Some 18 months after the revolution, in September 1980, the PRA comprised of approximately 305 soldiers in what was then termed the 'Combative' section, including a detachment at Carriacou, a service detachment which included a motor pool and an administrative element. An additional 145 soldiers, perhaps the only truly effective troops in the PRA, formed a Guard Company while an additional 39 personnel were abroad on training courses of various kinds.[36]

PRAF Troops on parade during the early years of the Revolution. (US National Archives)

New recruits to the PRAF undergoing training. (US National Archives)

PRAF troops marching to a parade ground. (US National Archives)

Of note is what may appear to be a substantial force of about 500 personnel was in reality only marginally a military force in any regard, with many personnel untrained and many more using obsolescent weapons from the Gairy era – when armed at all. However, a cadre of personnel had begun training in Cuba and Guyana and would soon allow for the expansion of the force into a reasonably effective small battalion-sized combat formation which was organised along Soviet/Cuban lines but without commensurate firepower because, as will be discussed, the PRAF could not absorb more weapons into its small establishment, much less provide them with trained crews.

The PRAF in theory comprised the PRA, the PRM and a small coast guard that consisted of converted fishing boats. The latter organisation was of negligible strength and even less value. There was no aviation element of any kind. The core strength revolved around a sub-strength infantry battalion which relied heavily on the reservists of the militia to bring it up to full strength.

Control of the PRAF was vested in the General Staff. This organisation was primarily responsible for military planning and for acting as a link between the field forces of the PRAF and the political/military secretary of the defence and interior, General Hudson Austin. General Austin was the only general officer of the PRAF and also held the portfolio of Minister of Communications, Works and Labour with the design and construction of the Point Salines Airport coming under his jurisdiction. As Secretary for Defence and Interior, Austin not only controlled the PRAF – for whose care and maintenance he was responsible – but also Grenada's increasingly powerful internal security forces.[38]

In contrast to Gairy's 'Green Beasts', the PRA had camps and centres around the island, including Camp Richardson, Camp Mitchell, Camp Villa, Camp Calivigny-Camp Fedon, Camp Williams, Camp Butler, Camp Blunt, Camp Boney, Camp Carriacou, Pearls Airport Camp, Grand Etang Lake Training Camp, Fort Rupert, Mount Royal, and Camp Allister-Fort Frederick. Some of these camps were temporary and others shifted location periodically but the PRA established a presence across the country, albeit reinforced by the PRM in due course. Of note is that some of these camps had detention centres which spoke to the far less salubrious role played by the PRA in enforcing the will of the PRG and silencing its opponents by all means at its disposal.[37]

The PRAF had a reasonably well-organised structure. The Grenadian General Staff divided the country – the main island and its smaller dependencies – into four military regions. Region I comprised the southwestern part of the main island, including the capital city of St. George's and the area around Point Salines. Region II comprised the east coast and the interior with its mountainous terrain. Region III comprised the northwestern part of the main

A BTR-60PB armoured personnel carrier of the PRA on manoeuvres in 1981. (US National Archives)

A BRDM-2 armoured reconnaissance vehicle of the PRA, after being captured by the USMC in 1983. (US National Archives)

island while Region IV encompassed Carriacou and Petite Martinique. These military regions ostensibly had PRM battalions assigned to them – two for Region I and one each for the other three regions.[39]

The PRAF was administered by the Ministry of Defence and Interior and had a small headquarters at the old True Blue barracks of Gairy's 'Green Beasts' which provided a degree of command and control over five elements, which were: the Unified Storeroom at Frequente with its two large warehouses, catering to all classes of supplies; the Unified Workshop which handled all equipment repair; the Medical Post to deal with all medical incidents; the Transportation Company which held most of the wheeled transport in the PRA (trucks, jeeps and motorcycles) and the farm on which the PRA and PRM grew food to supplement army rations and to reduce dependence on imported foodstuffs.

By 1983, on the eve of the tragic events of 19 October, the PRA had a personnel strength equivalent to that of a weak infantry battalion, with three company-sized units. The strongest of these was a motorised company with some 145 men at full strength – 91

Caption: PRAF troops with a M53 Quad 12.7mm AA gun. (US National Archives)

RPG rounds captured from the PRAF during Operation Urgent Fury. (US National Archives)

of whom were permanently assigned – which had at its disposal a force of eight BTR-60 APCs and two BRDM-2 scout cars. These were both equipped with 14.5mm heavy machine guns plus coaxial 7.62mm medium machine guns. With this armoured force, the PRA was better equipped than almost any country in the English-speaking Caribbean, with only Jamaica and Trinidad and Tobago then possessing any armoured vehicles and even then, they were of much less capability.[40]

Augmenting the motorised company was a mobile company with 150 men that was tasked with being a rapid response force, capable of moving anywhere on the island by truck. The PRA was rounded out by a small exploration company for reconnaissance with a strength of only 33 personnel, 24 of whom were from the militia and was the formation that replaced a rapid mobilisation company of the PRM, designed to take the field within 24 hours of notification but which had proved wholly incapable of that task.[41]

The PRA's permanent establishment was completed by an anti-aircraft battery, a logistics unit and several independent platoons assigned specifically for the security of the Ministry of Defence and Interior and the Unified Storeroom. Each security platoon, of which there were two, had a strength of 19 personnel, augmented by two independent anti-aircraft platoons, a Sappers/Engineering platoon, a transport platoon, a service platoon, a logistics unit and a communications platoon. Early in its existence, the PRA had a separate mortar platoon and a separate anti-tank platoon, but these were absorbed into the Motorised and Mobile companies of the PRA.[42]

Training of the PRA permanent force and other regular soldiers was done in both Grenada and abroad. Both Cuba and the Soviet Union provided instruction with several Grenadian personnel travelling to Cuba for military training. A much smaller number were sent to the Soviet Union for more advanced courses. Cuba maintained a small but permanent training team in Grenada, mainly of technical specialists while the Soviet Union and other Soviet bloc countries sent advisors on a temporary basis. These instructors were able create a nucleus of reasonably well-trained professional soldiers in the PRA but technical expertise remained in short supply. This was compounded by the propensity for Grenadian officers and NCOs to hold more than one position simultaneously, thus precluding developing experience in either.[43]

However, the troops of the PRA were able to attain a degree of competence with their individual and crew-served weapons. The PRA's anti-aircraft crews showed a good deal of competence while their anti-tank teams – equipped with RPG-2s, RPG-7s and 73 and 75mm recoilless rifles – showed much less (perhaps because none of the crews had ever seen a tank before). However, unit level training was poor as the Grenadian economy was too weak to support prolonged military exercises in the field.

The selection of certain officers for their political loyalty and sometimes expertise, without regard for leadership qualities, exacerbated the leadership problems in the PRA and did little to enable the force to become an effective fighting unit. Added to this was the indifferent level of education of many in the military – officers or enlisted personnel. While not illiterate, many of them had not graduated from secondary school which caused some additional difficulties in creating an effective military. For much of the army, and almost all of the PRM, instruction was largely theoretical and held in classrooms rather than in field exercises and, as was common in fledgling armies in small, communist states, that training consisted disproportionately of ideological conditioning

CPKF soldier with a captured RPG-2 and PKT light machine gun. (US National Archives)

The ZU-23-2 was the most potent air defence asset of the PRAF. This example was photographed after being captured during Operation Urgent Fury. (US National Archives)

rather than in practical military matters, with the result that even the PRA had problems functioning as a coherent military unit.[44]

If the PRA had its problems, then these were replicated manyfold in the PRM. In theory, the PRA was supported by the PRM with a notional strength of between two and three thousand. This was a chimera and the PRM was never as strong as the PRG wanted it to be and its personnel served more as a patriotic organisation than a military unit. The PRM was quite successful at promoting a sense of nationhood, and partially successful at promoting loyalty to the regime. Like many of its counterparts in the communist world, membership of the PRM was an important step in being able to obtain a secure job in the Grenadian public service.

In theory, the permanent force of the PRA was supported by five reserve battalions, each consisting of a nucleus of regular personnel but largely filled out with PRM troops. Organised as light infantry battalions, these units were wholly inadequate to do anything more than maintain internal security. Region I held the St. George's Battalion, with an authorised strength of 448 personnel, and the St. David's Battalion. Military Region II had the St. Andrew's Battalion, Region III had the St. Patrick's Battalion while Region IV had the Carriacou Battalion which had a theoretical strength of 256 but in practice only mustered some 150, little more than a reinforced rifle company. Equipment and training for the PRM was very poor with some weapons training taking place on an irregular basis. Training on crew-served weapons for the PRM was minimal and their combat performance was always viewed as dubious.[45]

Despite this less than formidable strength, before the overthrow of Bishop's government, the PRAF had completely delusional expansion plans that foresaw a massive expansion of the force from the existing one permanent infantry battalion and five reserve battalions to a force of three regular battalions and nine reserve battalions between 1983 and 1985. Wholly unrealistic plans included the acquisition of fifty BTR-152VI APCs, thirty 76mm ZiS-3 artillery pieces, thirty 57mm ZiS-2 anti-tank guns, 60 additional 82mm mortars, fifty Grad-P rocket launchers and four coastal patrol boats. Had this preposterous plan been implemented, one in four adult Grenadians would have been under arms by 1985. However, regular PRA officers were convinced that this plan would have never come to fruition and the equipment would have been largely confined to storage where it is likely it would have rusted away.[46] There has been speculation that these weapons could have been used to arm insurgent groups elsewhere in Latin America and the Caribbean, although it is unclear as to what use ZiS-3 and ZiS-2 artillery pieces – both long past their prime – would be to insurgents and the BTR-152 APC was long since obsolete and in very limited use worldwide. These arms plans were summarised as follows by the United States:

> The three Soviet agreements cited in this report provide for delivery between 1980 and 1986 of more than 1,000 pistols, more than 4,000 submachine guns, more than 90 portable rocket launchers, 7,000 land mines, 15,000 hand grenades and virtually all of Grenada's heavier artillery and heavier ammunition: 84 mortars, 400 heavy machine guns, 48 anti-aircraft guns, 50 GRAD-P howitzers [sic], 30 field guns, and 30 anti-tank guns. The agreements also furnish sixty armored personnel carriers and patrol vehicles, in addition to 86 other military-related vehicles, and some 14,000 uniforms.[47]

Yet Bishop's links to Cuba and the Soviet-bloc had earlier yielded rich dividends for weapons. In fact, following the US intervention, captured documents showed that the PRG received the following arms from Cuba in April 1979: 3,400 Soviet and US rifles, 200 light and medium machine guns, 100 rocket propelled grenades, 100 pistols and revolvers, twelve 82mm mortars, twelve 75mm recoilless rifles, twelve M53 quad 12.7mm anti-aircraft guns, over 3 million rounds of rifle ammunition, a half-million rounds for the machine guns, another 66,000 rounds for pistols, 4,000 rockets, 4,800 mortar shells, six hundred 75mm shells, and 237,000 rounds for the anti-aircraft guns.[48]

Of particular interest, and one which has not, perhaps, been sufficiently explored were the links between the Bishop's PRG and the Democratic People's Republic of Korea. According to captured documents:

> North Korea and Grenada announced a five-year development program during Prime Minister Bishop's trip to Pyongyang in April, 1983. According to the public announcement, North Korea would help build a 15,000-seat stadium, a party headquarters building, a fruit-processing factory, two fishing boats and an irrigation system.

North Korea would provide technical advisors and some construction materials and equipment, while Grenada would provide the bulk of the labor and materials and pay for the expenses of the technicians.

During that same visit to Pyongyang, however, Bishop concluded a secret military assistance agreement in which North Korea promised to supply small arms, ammunition and equipment to equip a force of more than 1,000 men. This equipment, listed in the formal agreement at a value of $12 million, was to include 1,000 assault rifles, 80 machine guns, 50 portable rocket launchers, 2 coast guard patrol boats, 6,000 uniforms, and large amounts of ammunition and other equipment.[49]

Captured PRAF anti-tank weapons including at least three 75mm and one 73mm SPG-9 recoilless rifles. (US National Archives)

The M53 quad 12.7mm anti-aircraft gun proved its worth during Urgent Fury. (US National Archives)

In 1983, however, none of this equipment had come. The reality of the PRAF was somewhat different and a far smaller and weaker force was available to the RMC. While the vast majority of the weapons planned for delivery were not supplied before Bishop's overthrow, years of Cuban and Soviet assistance had left its mark. The PRAF were small but far from poorly equipped for a force of its very modest size. It was a well-balanced force with theoretical combat potential beyond its mere numbers would seem to indicate and despite obvious deficiencies, performed reasonably well.

It should be noted, as will be detailed later, that the PRAF's mobilisation plans, which required the participation of the PRM in providing personnel for several key combat units, was completely compromised by the overthrow of Bishop, as at one stroke, the PRM became a potential foe for the RMC because of its strong connection to Bishop. The RMC could only rely on a small proportion of the PRM, seriously compromising the PRAF. This was particularly glaring in anti-aircraft units, where at least one critically important PRM battery was effectively unavailable as its crew refused to report for combat duty.

The PRAF was not badly equipped by regional standards and had been the beneficiary of substantial assistance from both Cuba and the Soviet bloc. Bishop's PRG, perhaps paranoid about an invasion, had created a substantial military for a small island. As has been noted, the PRA had a viable structure of three regular companies and a mobile company, augmented by reserve units and a security company. Ample weapons were available for this force.

Pride of place were the armoured vehicles of the motorised company consisting of eight BTR-60PB APCs and two BRDM-2 armoured cars. It should be noted that initial reporting in the aftermath of Urgent Fury accounted for either five or seven BTR-60s and one BRDM. One BTR-60 is known to have broken down before the start of hostilities. Infantry units had fire support in the form of ten 82mm mortars. Twelve such mortars were supplied by Cuba, but not all were available for issue because a lack of trained crews. There were also between eight and 12 recoilless rifles – at least two of which were 75mm Chinese Type 56 weapons with the anti-tank platoon – and others were 73mm SPG-9s. Infantry units had six RPG-7 and forty-six RPG-2 rocket launchers. While Cuba delivered a dozen 12.7mm machine guns for anti-aircraft defence, only six quad M53 12.7mm guns were brought into action against

Some of the 2,000 Moisin Nagants alongside other weapons captured in Grenada. (US National Archives)

Several Gairy-era weapons, including a number of obsolete rifles (rear right) with two AK-47s (rear left) and a PKT machine gun (foreground) captured in Grenada. (US National Archives)

the US. Anti-aircraft defences rested on twelve ZU-23-2 23mm towed anti-aircraft guns. Eighteen such guns were supplied by Cuba to the PRAF but a shortage of trained crews precluded the use of all 18 guns. Over 1,600 Kalashnikov assault rifles had been delivered along with over 4,000 SKS rifles, over 1,000 Czech Vz. 52/57 rifles and, surprisingly over 2,000 ancient Moisin Nagant rifles and some 200 Soviet-bloc submachine guns.[50]

These weapons augmented a not inconsiderable stock of weapons left over from Gairy's rule. Dozens of 0.303" Enfield rifles and submachine guns of the British Sten and American M3 types were available to the PRA and some of the latter were issued in combat. Support weapons available to the PRA infantry units were limited to PKM machine guns with a few 7.62mm L4A4 Bren guns from the Gairy era being available to the PRA, though their use in combat is unclear. The PRAF lacked artillery support, with only ten 82mm mortars being available. It should be noted that four ZiS-3 76mm guns were captured by American forces in Grenada. However, these were never issued to the PRAF and none of their personnel were trained to use such weapons.

Not surprisingly, only a small proportion of these weapons were actually issued for use in combat by PRAF personnel. Some of the remainder were used to arm the Cuban construction workers at Point Salines and the Cuban military advisors but there were many more weapons than personnel to use them, much less trained to use them competently. This was particularly true for anti-aircraft weapons and mortars. The PRAF was able to man only twelve ZU-23-2 and six M53 12.7mm guns and perhaps three to six of their 82mm mortars with trained crews. This had the effect of not only substantially reducing the number of anti-aircraft guns available for use against attacking aircraft, but the lack of crews precluded their use against ground targets in which they would have proved a formidable addition to the PRAF's arsenal. It should also be noted that the PRAF lacked any guided missiles for either anti-tank or anti-aircraft purposes and had no radar network. This would seriously hinder the PRAF's ability to engage incoming aircraft and would prove to be fatal.

At 0600 hours on 24 October 1983, one day before the start of Operation Urgent Fury, the regular element of PRAF mustered the modest strength of 463. This figure includes clerical and logistics personnel, prison guards, personal security officers of senior officials and administrative personnel from Regions I and II as well as the motorised company and the independent mobile company which were at less than full strength. It has been speculated that including its prison and police forces, the PRG could muster at most 906 regular personnel. With 463 answering the call to arms, it is clear that the response was not enthusiastic. Even this paled in comparison to the pathetic response of the PRM. With its loyalty to the PRG severely shaken by the murder of Bishop, only one in 10 of

Two Bren light machine guns, without their distinctive top-mounted curved magazines, from Gairy's era. (US National Archives)

A PRAF 82mm M37 mortar. (US National Archives)

the PRM, some 257 personnel in total, answered the call to arms. This total was augmented by the dubious addition of 58 untrained 'party comrades' who prepared to fight alongside the PRAF. In total, therefore, the PRAF managed to muster 778 personnel to repel an intervention by the armed forces of the Western hemisphere's superpower. It was a completely uneven match and the PRAF knew it.[51]

Cuban 'Forces'

The myth of large numbers of trained Cuban troops being present and fighting during Urgent Fury is one which has no basis in reality. Though the PRAF and the PRG had a long and fruitful relationship with the Cuban government and the Cuban armed forces, this did not translate into combat troops, nor any kind of a Cuban military intervention.

There were some 784 Cubans on the island with their breakdown, in detail, being as follows:

- 636 from the Ministry of Construction
- 17 from public health
- 12 from education
- 6 from agriculture
- 6 from transport
- 6 from the State Committee for Cooperation
- 5 from fishing
- 3 from basic industry
- 3 from culture
- 2 from domestic trade
- 1 from communications
- 1 from foreign trade
- 1 from the National Institute of Sports, Physical Education and Recreation
- 1 from Central Planning Board
- 43 from the Ministry of the Revolutionary Armed Forces (MINFAR): 22 officers and the rest translators and service personnel
- 9 from the Ministry of the Interior
- 12 comprising the twin crew and guards of an AN-26 plane that arrived at Grenville airport the day before the invasion
- 2 passengers on the plane: Colonel Pedro Tortoló, of MINFAR, who travelled to the island on a working visit, and Carlos Diaz, official of the Party Central Committee's America Department
- 18 from the diplomatic mission, including women and children
- Of the 784 Cubans, 44 were women[52]

While Colonel Pedro Tortoló Comas was dispatched by Castro to advise the RMC and act as an advisor, as has been, and will be, further detailed, Cuba's government was very reluctant to provide much by way of either advice or assistance to the RMC owning to the close personal friendship that had existed between Castro and Bishop. Of the 43 members of the MINFAR, most were technical advisors and not infantrymen though those who were, including Colonel Tortoló himself, were veterans of the Angolan war and were excellent soldiers.[53] The Cuban military advisors were deployed not only to assist the PRA to ready itself for combat, but also to organise the only marginally effective units available to Colonel Tortoló. It

Weapons captured at the Cuban compound including 82mm mortars and a 75mm recoilless rifle supplied by the PRAF. (US National Archives)

An Antonov An-26 medium transport belonging to Cubana. The aircraft arrived only a day before the US military intervention, and was captured intact at Pearls Airport. (US National Archives)

should also be noted, Tortoló arrived only hours before the first US troops landed.[54]

In terms of expectations, it is not entirely clear what Castro expected from Tortoló. While it might be anticipated that the Cuban military advisors would assist PRA and PRM units in combat, there was little time to prepare for a major US attack. Moreover, Tortoló had neither adequate staff nor material with which to do anything more than mount a token effort at defending their assigned positions. Whether Castro expected miracles or some suicidal bravery is not known but the Cubans were neither trained nor equipped nor motivated to do much to assist the RMC.

At Tortoló's disposal, in terms of available Cuban personnel, were only the 636 Cuban construction workers at Point Salines. As Cubans, they would have all served time as conscripts and had adequate knowledge of weapons to be potentially very effective soldiers in a defensive role. They were armed with assault rifles from PRA stocks and a few support weapons but no heavy weapons. Weapons made available to the Cubans were Kalashnikov assault rifles and RPK light machine guns with perhaps some PKM machine guns and RPGs being made available, along with some SPG-9s as well as possibly some Chinese 75mm recoilless rifles. At least one 12.7mm machine gun was available to the Cubans though whether it was used in the anti-aircraft role or in against ground targets is not clear. In theory, this was a battalion-sized unit with a reasonable degree of firepower.

In reality, despite their familiarity with weapons, the Cuban workers were neither prepared, nor trained nor motivated to fight any sort of action. This was of course handicapped by rules of engagement that were very restrictive plus their own antipathy to the RMC. It is also not clear what stocks of ammunition were made available to the Cubans to sustain resistance against the Americans. Grenada had ample stocks but in the confused and frantic planning prior to the US intervention, whether sufficient quantities had been moved to the Cuban positions is debatable. In fact, US reports in the aftermath of Operation Urgent Fury revealed that while the Cuban military regulars who fought alongside the PRA fought extremely well, the construction workers assigned to Point Salines had insufficient arms and ammunition to defend their positions against US forces.[55] This seems to suggest that whatever weapons from the PRA that were assigned to the Cubans were largely small arms such as rifles and pistols, with only a few machine guns and even fewer heavier weapons.

Despite all being former conscripts, most of the Cubans were recent arrivals to the island and many were middle-aged, with military training being in their distant past.[56] They had also never either organised or trained as a cohesive combat unit and, when combined with restrictive rules of engagement imposed upon them by Havana, their efficacy was completely compromised and, as will be shown, they offered minimal resistance against US forces.

It should also be noted that the Cuban government did nothing to augment the arsenal available to the RMC and the PRAF in the days leading up to Urgent Fury. It would have been simple, for example, to bring aboard the AN-26 that transported Colonel Tortoló, stocks of Strella-2M (SA-7) MANPADS or anti-tank guided missiles. While these would not have in themselves altered the outcome of the conflict, such weapons would have potentially inflicted many more casualties on the attacking American troops. It might be realistically said that the Cuban assistance to the RMC was minimal, grudging and largely symbolic. It also might be termed unnecessary and expensive.

In 1983 the PRA operated two types of armoured vehicles, both of Soviet design, both sourced from Cuba, and organized into a motorised company. The first of these were two BRDM-2 armoured scout cars with amphibious capability and each equipped with a 14.5mm KPVT heavy machine gun mounted in a small turret, with a 7.62mm PKT light machine gun installed coaxially. Armoured by between 5mm and 14mm steel plates (thicker at the front, thinner on sides and the rear), the BRDM-2 had a crew of four (driver, co-driver, commander, and gunner), a centralised tire-pressure regulation system, and a pair of chain-driven belly-wheels lowered by the driver, to enable trench-crossing. It could reach speeds of up to 100km/h (62mph) on roads. Both of the vehicles operated by the PRA were painted in dark green overall and are not known to have worn any kind of markings. (Artwork by David Bocquelet)

The second type of Soviet-designed armoured vehicle operated by the motorised company of the PRA was the BTR-60PB, eight of which were available. At 5-9mm thickness, the armour of this eight-wheeled armoured personnel carrier only provided protection from small arms fire and shell splinters. The turret was exactly the same as that installed on the BRDM-2 and included the 14.5mm KPVT heavy machine gun, with a 7.62mm PKT light machine gun installed coaxially. The crew of three consisted of the driver, commander, and gunner, and the passenger compartment could take up to eight fully armed troops. Painted in dark green overall, Grenadian BTR-60s seem to have worn small 'serial numbers' applied near the centre of the superstructure: this one was '028'. (Artwork by David Bocquelet)

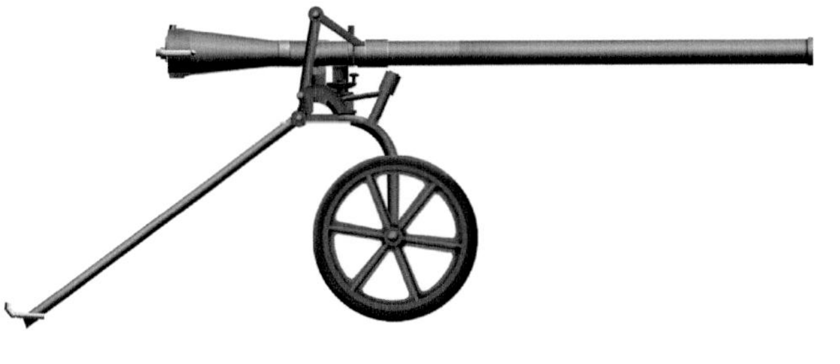

Amongst the most potent artillery pieces of the PRA were 18 towed 23mm ZU-23-2 anti-aircraft guns (left), and twelve 75mm recoilless rifles unspecified type (right). Both presented a potent threat against soft-skin and lightly armoured vehicles of the US Marine Corps in particular, and the ZU-23-2 was potentially dangerous for US helicopters and low-flying aircraft. However, the Grenadians had only 12 trained crews for the former, and even fewer for the latter. Unsurprisingly, both types saw only minimal action. As far as is known, the ZU-23s and recoilless rifles retained their olive drab overall livery, as applied before delivery. (Artworks by David Bocquelet)

The Landing Vehicle, Tracked, Personnel-7 (LVTP-7) – later renamed to the Amphibious Assault Vehicle (AAVP-7A1) – is a fully tracked amphibious landing vehicle and the primary armoured personnel carrier of the US Marine Corps during Operation Urgent Fury. This eight-metre-long, 30-ton vehicle had a crew of three (driver, commander, and gunner), could carry up to 21 fully-armed Marines, and was armed with 12.7mm M2HB heavy machine gun. The 22nd MAU deployed 13 LVTP-7s – all of which wore the MERDC camouflage – for its amphibious landing in the Grand Mal Bay, on the first day of the war. (Artwork by David Bocquelet)

The heaviest armoured vehicle to see action during Operation Urgent Fury were five M60A1 tanks of 3rd Platoon of A Company, 2nd Tank Battalion, four of which were involved in the landing at Grand Mal Bay. They saw action while relieving the Navy SEALs the following morning, enabling the evacuation of Governor Scoon, his family and aides. Weighting about 51 tons, the M60A1 had sloped armour with an effective thickness of approximately 250mm on the front, was armed with an M68 105mm gun (a licenced version of the famous British L7 gun), one 7.62mm machine gun installed coaxially, and a single 12.7mm M85 heavy machine gun in the commander's cupola. As standard for most US military vehicles of the early 1980s, all were painted in the MERDC camouflage, including a complex pattern consisting of dark green (FS34102), field drab (FS30118), sand (FS30277) or white, and black. (Artwork by David Bocquelet)

The Ford M151 ¼-ton 4x4 truck was the successor to the famous M38 and M38A1 jeep Light Utility Vehicles from the times of the Korean war. Its design included an integrated box frame and sheet-steel body, providing more space, and all-around independent suspension with coil springs, providing better ground clearance. Introduced to service in the early 1960s, it played an active part in all US military operations well into the 1980s, by when the most-widely used variant was the M151A2, with improved rear suspension (allowing the transportation of heavier loads). Most were not armed, but during the Urgent Fury, many M151s carried a pintle-mounted machine gun, while some carried launchers for BGM-71 TOW anti-tank guided missiles, as illustrated here. (Artwork by David Bocquelet)

Unlike other US Army troops involved in Operation Urgent Fury, Rangers from the 2/75th Ranger Battalion were easily distinguishable by wearing Vietnam-era fatigues, including M1951 Patrol Caps or M1 steel helmets, and Tropical Combat Boots. The web gear was from the ALICE system, while the rucksack in this case was used to carry ammunition for the M67 recoilless rifle, which was somewhat obsolete by the early 1980s. His personal firearm was the 5.56mm CAR-15 (a lightweight carbine based upon the M16), and .45 ACP M1911 pistol. (Artwork by Anderson Subtil)

Amongst the members of the Eastern Caribbean Defence Force was a small contingent of the Royal Police Force of Saint Vincent and the Grenadines, drawn from the Special Service Unit (SSU). They wore Jamaican made uniforms, large black berets without insignia, and US-made tropical combat boots. The webbing equipment probably corresponded to the British 1958 Pattern. Unlike other Caribbean contingents, which used British firearms (mainly SLR assault rifles), he was armed with FN FAL assault rifle of Belgian origin. (Artwork by Anderson Subtil)

This machine-gunner of the 82nd Airborne Division is shown wearing the ripstop fabric BDU uniform and All-Purpose Lightweight Individual Carrying Equipment (ALICE). His helmet is of the Personal Armor System for Ground Troops design (PASGAT), introduced on a large scale shortly before Operation Urgent Fury, manufactured of Kevlar and commonly referred to as the 'Fritz' due to its similarity to the German Stahlhelm of the Second World War. His firearm is a 7.62mm M60 machine gun, the main squad-level support weapon of the US Army infantry of the time. (Artwork by Anderson Subtil)

The centrepiece of the flying component of the 22nd MAU during Operation Urgent Fury was Marine Medium Helicopter Squadron 261 (HMM-261) 'Raging Bulls'. As of 1983, the unit was equipped with the large and powerful Sikorsky CH-53D Sea Stallion heavy-lift helicopter, which originally entered service in the mid-1960s. The D version was powered by uprated T64-GE-413 engines, had an improved transmission and a revised interior, enabling transportation of up to 55 troops. Four were embarked on board USS *Guam* (LPH-9), all painted in olive drab overall, and wearing only toned-down markings, including the unit insignia on the rear of the gearbox cover, service title and national marking on the rear of the fuselage, and the tailfin code (EM). (Artwork by Luca Canossa)

During Operation Urgent Fury, the centrepiece of HMM-261 were Boeing-Vertol CH-46E Sea Knight twin-engined helicopters. All were painted in olive drab, and wore only toned-down insignia, including the code EM, their AerNo, and the unit crest on the rear engine cowling, service title, modex number and unit designation along the upper side of the cabin, national insignia low on the forward cabin, and the modex on the nose. They participated in deploying troops of 2nd Battalion, 8th Marines to the island, evacuated the surviving crewmember of a downed AH-1 Cobra, and then carried infantry from the 75th Ranger Regiment to conduct the evacuation of US students from the Grand Anse campus. This is a reconstruction of the unlucky CH-46E AerNo 157711/EM00, which crashed after colliding with a palm tree, and was then destroyed by an AC-130. (Artwork by Pablo Albornoz)

The combat component of HMM-261 during Operation Urgent Fury included four Bell AH-1T Sea Cobras, which were armed with the powerful, three-barrel 20mm M197 cannon installed in a turret under the chin, and two each of LAU-3 and LAU-12 pods for Mk66 HYDRA 68mm unguided rockets. They wore the usual tailfin code of the 22ND MAU – EM – but were reinforced by at least two examples from HML-167, which wore the tailfin codes TV. All were painted in olive drab overall and wore only toned-down markings. This example, AH-1T AerNo 160801 was drawn from the HML-167. (Artwork by Tom Cooper)

As usual for all MAUs of the 1980s, during its Atlantic Ocean and Mediterranean Sea cruise on board USS *Guam*, HMM-261 included a utility component consisting of four Bell UH-1N Twin Huey helicopters. First flown in 1969, this was a stretched-fuselage variant of the venerable Bell 205/UH-1 family, powered by a PT6T-3/T400 Turbo Twin Pac made up of two Pratt & Whitney Canada PT6 power sections that drove a single output shaft. The USMC modified its UH-1Ns with a stability augmentation system, which resulted in the removal of the well-known 'stabilisation bar' on top of the main rotor head. Whenever necessary, Twin Hueys were armed with pintle-mounted machine guns, as illustrated here. All four of HMM-261's UH-1Ns were painted in olive drab overall and wore toned-down insignia including national markings and service title on the boom, and a two-digit modex number on the doors. (Artwork by Luca Canossa)

Introduced to service with the 101st Combat Aviation Brigade of the 101st Airborne Division from June 1979 to replace the venerable Bell UH-1, the Sikorsky UH-60 Black Hawk was still a brand-new sight within the US armed forces at the time of Operation Urgent Fury. Indeed, the intervention in Grenada was its baptism of fire. The mass of the Black Hawks were of the UH-60A variant, which had a crew of four, the capacity to carry 11 fully-equipped troops, and was usually armed with a pair of M134 miniguns installed in the windows behind the cabin. All were drawn from the 82nd and 101st Combat Aviation Brigades, painted in olive drab overall, and wore a bare minimum of markings, including only service titles and (usually next to invisible) serials applied on the fin. (Artwork by Pablo Albornoz)

In addition to UH-60As used for assault, liaison, and utility purposes, the US Army employed a number of UH-60M Black Hawks of the 57th Medical Detachment (not to be mistaken for the significantly improved UH-60M Upgrade Black Hawk, introduced to service starting in 1987). Like UH-60As, they had no stub-wings for drop tanks, and instead of armament were equipped with medical mission equipment, including six stretchers for casualties. All were painted in the same olive drab as the UH-60As, but wore large red crosses applied on the cabin doors and nose. (Artwork by Pablo Albornoz)

AC-130H Spectre gunships of the 16th Special Operations Squadron, USAF, were in action right from the start of Operation Urgent Fury. Home-based at Hurlburt Field in Florida, they were forward deployed at Bridgetown Airport in Barbados. Tasked with armed reconnaissance and close air support, they provided last-moment intelligence for the air assault forces, and then silenced numerous anti-aircraft emplacements, especially around Point Salines airfield. While some might have worn the Europe One camouflage pattern, most seem to have been painted in an overall gunship grey livery as of 1983 (confirmed for 69-6569, 69-6567 and 656574). Other AC-130E/Hs known to have been deployed in support of Operation Urgent Fury included 6965-70 ('The Hussy'), 69-6572 ('Grave Digger'), 69-6573 ('Heavy Metal'), 69-6574 ('Iron Maiden'), 69-6575 ('Wicked Wanda') and 69-6577 ('Death Angel'). (Artwork by Tom Cooper)

The EC-130E Commando Solo was a variant of this prolific family of transport aircraft, equipped for psychological operations and modified through the addition of equipment from the retired EC-121S Coronet Solo aircraft. It entered service with the US Air Force in 1978. After two reorganisations of the fleet, in 1983 all the aircraft were handed over to the 193rd Special Operations Wing of the Pennsylvania Air National Guard, subjected to the Air Force Special Operations Command. During Operation Urgent Fury, EC-130Es of the 193rd Special Operations Group acted as airborne radio stations, informing the people of Grenada of the US military action. As far as is known, at the time all wore the South East Asia camouflage pattern in tan (FS30219), dark green-brown (FS34079), and green (FS34102) on upper surfaces and sides, and light grey (FS36622) on undersides. (Artwork by Tom Cooper

Cubana, the national airline of Cuba, acquired a total of 12 Antonov An-24RVs in the 1970s, followed by 20 more powerful An-26s in the 1980s. The type served primarily for domestic transport, but was sometimes used for flying to Barbados, Mexico, Nicaragua, and Panama. This example – registered as CU-T1254 – had the bad luck of being used to bring in Cuban workers to Grenada on 24 October 1983. Because Point Salines Airport was closed for construction work, it landed at Pearl Airport – where it was subsequently found and captured by US troops, together with an An-2. By the early 2010s, both were still in place, and falling apart due to corrosion caused by the elements. (Artwork by Tom Cooper)

The Ling-Temco-Vought (LTV) A-7E Corsair II was the primary light attack aircraft of the US Navy in the 1970s and 1980s, and two squadrons were embarked on every aircraft carrier. In the case of USS *Independence* during the Atlantic Ocean and Mediterranean Sea cruise of 1983, these were VA-87 and VA-15. The aircraft shown here was assigned to the latter unit, nick-named the Valions, which was one of the first to operate this type in 1969. The jet is shown wearing the tactical paint scheme in medium grey (FS36320) on top surfaces and sides and light grey (FS36375) on undersides, toned-down markings, and armed with a Mk.20 Rockeye CBU (outboard pylon) and Mk.82 general-purpose bomb (inboard pylon) – which was a typical weapons configuration during Operation Urgent Fury. (Artwork by Tom Cooper)

The second A-7E squadron of USS *Independence* during Operation Urgent Fury was VA-87 Golden Warriors, established in 1968 as the first fleet squadron for this type. At least since converting to the improved A-7E variant, in 1976, the unit operated some of most colourful Corsairs: by 1983, such times were over, and most of the aircraft were repainted in the tactical paint scheme described above: only the jets nominally assigned to the commander of Carrier Air Wing 6 (modex AE400, shown here) and the commanding officer of VA-87 (modex AE401) were left in gull gray (FS16440) on top surfaces and sides, and white (FS17875) on undersurfaces. This jet is illustrated as armed with a total of eight Mk.82 250kg general purpose bombs (three installed on a multiple-ejector-rack on outboard underwing pylon, and one on the centre underwing pylon). (Artwork by Tom Cooper)

The third attack squadron assigned to Carrier Air Wing 6, embarked on USS *Independence*, and involved in Operation Urgent Fury was the VA-176 Thunderbolts. Established in 1955, this unit converted to Grumman A-6A Intruders in 1969 and made 18 deployments to the Mediterranean Sea by 1991. As usual by 1983, most of its aircraft (except for four KA-6D tankers) were painted in the tactical paint scheme including grey (FS35237) on upper surfaces and sides and medium grey (FS36320) on undersides – which tended to rapidly deteriorate due to heavy wear and the elements. All markings and national insignia were applied in medium grey (FS36320). This example is shown armed with a pair of Mk.20 Rockeye cluster bomb units, installed on a multiple ejector rack under the inboard underwing pylon. (Artwork by Tom Cooper)

(Map by Anderson Subtil)

5
PLANNING URGENT FURY

US Atlantic Command, under the able leadership of Admiral Wesley L. MacDonald, was responsible for the planning of Operation Urgent Fury. The events in Grenada came as a surprise and the operation had to be organised at extremely short notice and with minimal information on opposing forces. Furthermore, a lack of clarity was evident as to what the objective of any military intervention might be. However, the US Joint Chiefs of Staff, headed by General John W. Vessey Jr., would later write:

> We, the JCS, followed our interpretation of the lessons of Desert One and of the broader allegations of weaknesses in the system during the Grenada operation. (1) We gave the task to the commander responsible for the territory. (2) The JCS, personally reviewed the CINCLANT plan, agreed on its weaknesses and directed the commander to come up with a new plan. [...] (3) The SecDef personally reviewed the plan and approved it; he also had all of the JCS go with him and the Chairman to brief the President on the plan. The President personally queried each of the JCS about their support for the plan before approving it, himself. (4) The President and the SecDef personally reviewed the plan a second time before ordering its execution. The execution of the plan was then in the hands of the Unified Commander. The SecDef and the President did not interfere, but the SecDef was repeatedly briefed on progress. I had SecDef's authority to supervise execution of the plan, but only within the context of the plan he had approved.[1]

One of the biggest challenges faced by the United States, other than the practical ones of arranging a military operation at very short notice, was that the United States was faced with the prospect of a hostage rescue operation where over 600 American students (some suggest over 700) and some 400 nationals of friendly foreign countries were potentially at risk. The United States had no knowledge of the fate of these persons after the events of 19 October and could not have known that Castro had warned the RMC against using the foreigners as hostages. Furthermore, the United States would have been concerned about the safety of the Governor General, Sir Paul Scoon, who may have been at risk. Thus, part of the planning had to involve a hostage rescue component and, as the Chairman of the JCS noted, the lessons of the failed Iranian hostage rescue operation and the fiasco of Desert One were fresh in their minds. This meant that planning to rescue the students and the Governor General had to be meticulous and to cater for unforeseen resistance, with redundancy built into the endeavour.

However, this mission was soon expanded and after the murder of Prime Minister Bishop and members of his Cabinet – plus the deaths of many Grenadian civilians as they tried to rescue them – saw the rescue mission expanded quite significantly. As historian Robert H. Cole would write:

> State Department evacuation planning rapidly shifted to Department of Defense (DOD) planning for a much larger military operation. Uncertain of the strength of the Grenadian troops and armed Cuban workers, US Atlantic Command (USLANTCOM) planners developed a wide range of courses of action and recommended a large joint task force (JTF) to overwhelm the opposition.
>
> In a 20 October meeting, Secretary of State George P. Shultz and the Chairman of the Joint Chiefs of Staff, General John W. Vessey, Jr., USA, warned the Special Situation Group (SSG) comprised of Vice President George Bush and other top national security advisors that the Grenadian junta might resist an evacuation and that armed Cuban construction workers might intervene. The SSG approved a recommendation by the Chairman that the mission be expanded to include neutralization of Grenadian forces and the armed Cuban workers and reconstruction of the Grenadian government.

The centrepiece of the US Navy during the 1980s were the supercarriers, up to of which 16 were available, but 14 operational on average. Operation Urgent Fury was supported by the Carrier Battle Group centred on USS *Independence* (CV-62) and including the guided-missile cruiser USS *Richmond K Turner* (CG-20), guided-missile destroyer USS *Coontz* (DDG-40), destroyers USS *Caron* (DD-970), USS *Moosbrugger* (DD-980), guided-missile frigate USS *Clifton Sprague* (FFG-16), and replenishment ship USS *Suribachi* (AE-21). (US DoD)

A-7E Corsair IIs of attack squadrons VA-15 and VA-87 parked on the forward deck of USS *Independence*. (US DoD)

The island of USS *Independence*, with aircraft of Carrier Air Wing 6 around it. Constructed to the *Forrestal*-class design, USS *Independence* was commissioned to service in January 1959, and could embark up to 90 combat aircraft. (US DoD)

Following presidential approval of an expanded mission, GEN Vessey made two far-reaching decisions. To ensure maximum operational security, he imposed special category (SPECAT) restrictions on all planning message traffic; this limited planning information to selected members of the Intelligence (J2) and Operations (J3) Directorates. Vessey then approved the course of action which specified a coup de main in which Rangers or Marines and airborne troops would conduct multiple simultaneous rescue and combat operations. After the diversion of US warships to Grenada became news on 21 October, US intelligence agencies reported that the Grenadians and Cubans were organizing to resist. The President then approved the Chairman's recommendation that the US ground forces include both Rangers and Marines.[2]

While the events of 19 October gave the United States the excuse for an expanded mission, the fears for its nationals should not be understated. Students, faced with a four-day 24-hour curfew and with a closed airport, found themselves having to violate curfews merely to get food and water. It also prevented any of the thousand foreign nationals on the island from leaving the country. In retrospect, had the airport not been closed and assurances given to foreign nationals, at least some of the excuses used by the United States to expand the mission would have disappeared. However, in the event, Admiral MacDonald was given his directive by the JCS at 1654 hours on 22nd October 1983 which directed him to:

> … conduct military operations to protect and evacuate US and designated foreign nationals from Grenada, neutralize Grenadian forces, stabilize the internal situation, and maintain the peace. In conjunction with OECS/friendly government participants, assist in the restoration of a democratic government in Grenada.[3]

One might summarise the US operation as being one where the US would strike hard and fast. They would present the international community with a *fait accompli*. Their forces would enter Grenada, crush all opposition, get US citizens out and hand the job over to a force of Caribbean peacekeepers who would then aid in the reestablishment of democratic government in Grenada.[4]

Intervention Options

After receiving requests from the OECS and, apparently, Sir Paul Scoon, on 21 October 1983, all plans for a peaceful evacuation of US nationals were abandoned and a far more robust intervention was now envisaged. US planning, as described by the JCS history of the operation noted:

> With two separate requests for intervention in hand, the NSPG jettisoned the idea of a peaceful evacuation. The NSPG tasked the Joint Chiefs of Staff to plan a military expedition to seize Grenada from local military forces. Anticipating such an order, the Joint Staff had prepared alternative force packages: either two battalions of Rangers with JSOC elements or a Marine battalion landing team with SEALs totaling about eighteen hundred men. Either package would be reinforced with a follow-on force of at least two airborne battalions.
>
> The concept for employing JSOC elements and the Rangers called for five specially equipped C-130s to drop JSOC teams under cover of darkness at Point Salines at the southwest tip of Grenada and at Pearls midway up the east coast. Protected by four helicopter gunships, the commandos would seize the airfields. From Point Salines, some of them would then move up the west coast about four miles to St. George's, the island capital, and capture the radio station and police headquarters. These forces would then move about four miles southeast to capture the Grenadian military barracks at Calivigny. Later, sixteen C-130s would land the 1st and 2nd Ranger Battalions at Point Salines and Pearls. They would consolidate control of all objectives and pursue any enemy forces fleeing into the highlands. The Joint Staff estimated that up to four and a half hours would be required to seize control of all objectives. To begin the operation on the night of 25 October, the earliest possible date, a presidential decision would be required by 2000 hours on 22 October.
>
> The second concept, an amphibious/heliborne assault by Marines with a Ranger follow-up force, used more manpower, but could be executed several hours earlier. Teams of SEALs would go ashore after midnight on 24 October to reconnoiter beach conditions at Point Salines and Pearls. By dawn of 25 October, a battalion landing team with air cover from the USS *Independence* would either land on the beaches or move by helicopter to objectives at Point Salines airfield, the St. George's medical school, and the Grand Anse beach about two miles below St. George's. Deploying to the east of Grand Anse, the Marines would then seize the Calivigny barracks. Once the Marines had secured their objectives, Rangers could land at Point Salines and move to St. George's to seize police headquarters, government buildings, and army headquarters.[5]

Rather shockingly, the United States had a wholly inflated impression of the opposing forces. One estimate suggested that the Cuban ship *Vietnam Heroica* might have carried 240 Cuban combat troops to Grenada. They estimated that the PRA had some 1,200 regular troops augmented by up to 5,000 PRM reservists. These figures had no bearing in reality.[6] However, the JCS rightly appreciated that Grenada was too far away for any Soviet assistance to the RMC and that Cuban involvement might include some reinforcement of the Grenadian PRA but that the Cuban Navy,

An elevated view of USS *Guam* in the early 1980s. Essentially a helicopter carrier, this class had no ability to land troops by other means. Therefore, the embarked troops were only lightly equipped and served as an advance echelon. In turn, and like other vessels of the Iwo Jima-class, USS *Guam* generally operated in conjunction with other amphibious assault ships, such as amphibious transport docks (LPDs), dock landing ships (LSDs), and landing ship tanks (LSTs), which carried heavier equipment and additional troops. (US DoD)

despite being large by Caribbean standards – with submarines, missile boats, and torpedo carrying hydrofoils – would be incapable of providing any assistance of any value to the RMC. The Cuban Air Force was not considered a factor, though it might wish to disrupt the US concentration of force. The MiG-23s of the FAR were not in a position to contest either air superiority or conduct any offensive operations to hinder the US deployment.

This completely bizarre appreciation of the opposing force is indicative of both a complete lack of human intelligence and effective appreciation of the ground situation in Grenada as well as a desire by some in the US establishment to inflate the threat that was faced by the US in Grenada. It is one of the abiding mysteries of America's involvement in the Caribbean that its knowledge and understanding of ground realities in the region, as well its appreciation of its opposition – whether military or ideological – was and remains exceedingly poor. This inflated its perception of the military opposition in Grenada.

Given their concerns about opposition force levels, the United States planned to commit a substantial number of troops to ensure their ability to overwhelm any resistance in a matter of days, rather than weeks or months. They thus planned an attack where surprise and overwhelming force would prove decisive. As Cole would write:

> Given the uncertainty, the JCS determined that a military operation should be a coup de main, that is, a surprise attack with overwhelming force. While catching the enemy off guard, such an operation could perform rescue missions and seize key military targets vital to the enemy's command and control of defensive operations. Forces substantially larger than the one available Marine battalion landing team of eighteen hundred men would be required. Earmarking the Marines for an amphibious assault to take one airfield, the Joint Chiefs decided to employ Rangers to seize the other airfield. Troops from the 82nd Airborne Division would provide reinforcements.[7]

Critical to the planning process was the concern that the operation might backfire and produce adverse consequences, both in respect of the lives of US nationals in Grenada and in respect of US global prestige and raise issues over the possible breaches of international law. The loss of prestige would be compounded if the PRAF and Cubans inflicted significant casualties on attacking US forces. The latter point was particularly sensitive as this would be the first operation since the Vietnam War debacle. There was a desire in the US to re-establish its military credibility as a reliable ally. As the official JSC history notes, in respect of the two main options for military action:

> Either option had risks. Landings by Rangers or Marines might prompt the Grenadians or Cubans to kill the students or hold them hostage. The Cuban construction workers might reinforce Grenadian troops and inflict significant casualties upon US forces; the Soviet Union might exert pressure on US forces or those of US allies in Europe or the Middle East. If any of those events occurred, the Reagan administration could expect criticism from Congress, the media, and foreign governments. Some critics would focus on the casualties or hostages; others might accuse the President of disregard for international law.
>
> The Joint Staff concluded that the rewards of a successful operation offset the risks. A swift, precise strike probably would rescue most of the students and avert a hostage situation. Removal of the pro-Cuban junta would eliminate a threat to US strategic interests in the Caribbean. A well-executed display of US military prowess would convey US determination to protect its vital interests. In Western Europe where US willingness to fight for European soil was questioned, such action might inspire confidence in the United States.[8]

The clinching step that effectively activated the US intervention was the RMC's attempt to recall the entire PRM to arms – believed by the US to add another 2,000 troops to Grenada's military. This, with the over 1,200 PRA regulars and over 600 armed Cubans, would theoretically give the PRAF some 4,000 personnel with which to resist any intervention. A force of this size would inevitably pose a significant challenge to any small hostage rescue operation in Grenada. To this end:

> According to GEN Vessey, the Joint Chiefs of Staff wanted "to go in with enough force absolutely to get the job done [...] to minimize casualties, both on our side and on theirs. We wanted to intimidate the Cubans." Accordingly, the NSPG directed the Joint Chiefs to send an execute order to ADM McDonald authorizing him to land a multi-service force of JSOC, Rangers, Marines and airborne troops, on Grenada on 25 October. The presidential decision to use military action authorized ADM McDonald to organize a joint force with the missions of evacuating US citizens, disarming hostile forces, and restoring orderly government to Grenada. It also directed USCINCRED and CINCMAC to provide additional ground forces and transport planes. If, within twenty hours of receipt of the execute order, danger to the US citizens on the island had significantly increased, ADM McDonald was free to launch an immediate rescue using JSOC teams flown in by C-130.
>
> Shortly after dispatch of the execute order, GEN Vessey alerted CINCSAC that his command would support the operation. CINCSAC immediately ordered the Director of Tanker Operations to assemble KC-135 and KC-10 tanker aircraft at Robbins Air Force 27 Base, Georgia, and Roosevelt Roads Naval Air Station (NAS), Puerto Rico, to refuel aircraft used during the operation. He also prepared to support USCINCLANT with airborne reconnaissance and monitoring missions in the eastern Caribbean. Starting on 22 October, GEN Vessey communicated with ADM McDonald primarily by secure telephone. In the course of these conversations, the Chairman stressed the JCS belief that the size of the joint force planned by the LANTCOM staff did not appear adequate to intimidate and overwhelm the enemy. Vessey urged McDonald to revise his plan to increase the size of the force "to do the job quickly," and to request any additional forces needed.
>
> At this point, DIA provided the JCS with a revised estimate of Grenadian capacity and will to resist. Estimating Grenadian strength at no more than fifteen hundred regulars and three thousand reservists, DIA analysts expected the Grenadian forces to mount a determined resistance. The analysts also pointed out the presence of at least six Soviet-made armored personnel carriers (BTR 60s) and four Soviet-made 23mm antiaircraft guns (ZU-23s), most of which were believed to be sited around the Cuban construction site at the Point Salines runway. Analysts, however, expected little resistance from the nearly six hundred Cuban construction workers and fifty Cuban military advisers believed to be on the island.[9]

A view from the bridge of USS *Guam* towards the bow, with (from front to rear), one AH-1T Cobra attack helicopter and six CH-46E Sea Knight assault helicopters. (US DoD)

The United States, however, despite its vast power, would require significant assistance to complete its desired operations. Not the least of these would be the need for the United States to persuade the OECS, Barbados and Jamaica to participate in the subsequently-envisaged Caribbean Peacekeeping Force but also the need to have these countries, in particular Barbados, provide logistical support for the US force. This was to be of particular importance because of the need for helicopter support for the Special Operation Forces of Joint Task Force 123, which was needed to conduct the hostage rescue operation. While some units could fly directly from the United States, the helicopters of TF 160 would not have the range to conduct such a flight and as such their transport to a neighbouring island and their subsequent assembly for operations would need to be done at short notice.

Finally, after considering all options and possibilities, there was a final National Security Decision Directive (NSDD):

> The draft NSDD spelled out a three-fold mission: rescue of US citizens, restoration of democratic government, and preclusion of Cuban interference. For execution of military operations in support of the mission, the NSDD assigned primary responsibility to the Secretary of Defense, but directed him to coordinate political aspects of the mission with the Secretary of State and the Director of Central Intelligence. The Secretary of State was to arrange diplomatic cooperation with the OECS, Jamaica, and Barbados; to inform the Soviet Union and Cuba, at the proper time, of plans to protect and evacuate their nationals; and to prepare a campaign to convince Congress and the public that the operation was truly multilateral, that the current regime threatened US lives, and that the next Grenadian government would be more democratic.[10]

Organising the Intervention

The JCS history on Operation Urgent Fury divides the US intervention into four distinct phases:

> In Phase 1, "Transit," the *Independence* battle group and MARG 1-84 would close to positions fifty-five nautical miles northwest and forty nautical miles north of Grenada. Six hours before the invasion, JSOC teams and Rangers would fly out of Pope Air Force Base, North Carolina, and Hunter Army Airfield, Georgia.
>
> Phase 2, "Insertion," required heliborne and seaborne insertions of special operations forces several hours before dawn to conduct final reconnaissance, strike at critical Grenadian police and military installations in the St. George's area, and move to the Governor General's residence to protect him.
>
> Meanwhile, battalions of Rangers and Marines would capture the airfields at Point Salines and Pearls. At this stage, URGENT FURY was seen as primarily an unconventional operation to evacuate civilians with a strong force of Rangers and Marines to deter outside interference. If Grenadians or Cubans attempted to block evacuation, the Rangers and Marines would respond as required by the situation. As backup, the 82nd Airborne Division at Fort Bragg, North Carolina, would go on full alert three hours before H-hour. Admiral McDonald's guidance to the task force reflected concern that the invasion be conducted with precision to minimize civilian casualties and damage to the local economy and infrastructure.

During Operation Urgent Fury, USS *Guam* was the centrepiece of a Marine amphibious assault group including USS *Barnstable County* (LST-1197), USS *Manitowoc* (LST-1180), USS *Fort Snelling* (LSD-30), and USS *Trenton* (LPD-14). This photograph shows USS *Trenton* underway in the Atlantic Ocean in 1986. (US DoD)

Phases 3 and 4 of the concept were known as "Stabilization/Evacuation" and "Peacekeeping," respectively. In Phase 3, after forces had secured airfields and key military and government installations, they would locate and protect US citizens, Governor General Scoon, and foreigners, including those from communist countries. Evacuation of civilians set the stage for Phase 4, "Peacekeeping." Admiral McDonald's plan excluded the untrained OECS constabulary from assault landings. Instead, MAC would fly the three hundred-man force from Jamaica and Barbados to Grenada to work with the US force and the Governor General to establish the interim government.

Admiral McDonald proposed that Vice Admiral Metcalf, as Commander of the Second Fleet, command the invasion force. On D-Day, VADM Metcalf would command four task forces known collectively as Combined Joint Task Force (CJTF) 120. Task Force 123, also known as "the JSOC/Rangers Task Force," included JSOC teams, pilots and crews of the 160th Aviation Battalion from Fort Campbell, Kentucky, and two battalions of Army Rangers. Task Force 124 comprised an amphibious group made up of several ships including the flagship of VADM Metcalf, the USS *Guam*, and a battalion landing team of Marines from the 22nd Marine Amphibious Unit.

Task Force 126 included a detachment of eight F-15s from the 33rd Tactical Fighter Wing and four E-3As from the 552nd Airborne Warning and Control System (AWACS) Detachment. Task Force 126's principal mission would be to prevent interference by Cuban vessels or aircraft. Task Force 121, made up of the 2nd and 3rd Brigades and support units of the 82nd Airborne Division, would land on Grenada about nine hours after the initial assaults and then take charge of the Rangers and other Army units. To support CJTF 120, VADM Metcalf had the ships and planes of the *Independence* battle group as well as elements from SAC, MAC, and USREDCOM. In the USLANTCOM concept, the SAC and MAC aircraft would operate independently of Task Force 126.[11]

The final preparation for Operation Urgent Fury began with an attempt to plug gaps in Joint Task Force 123's tactical intelligence. Two C-130s dropped two SEAL teams – one at Point Salines and one at Pearls. The team at Pearls came ashore and indicated that conditions did not favour an amphibious landing and recommended a heliborne operation. The team for Point Salines vanished in rough seas. However, all the preliminary work was completed and with forces in place – with C-5 Galaxies bringing TF 160's helicopters to Grantley Adams Airport in Barbados – D-Day was set for 0500 hours, 25 October 1983.

Challenges Faced in Preparing the Intervention Force

The preparation of any operation at short notice inevitably creates challenges and despite its formidable capabilities, the United States was no exception. Indeed, many issues were found in the early stages of planning where several logistics experts were excluded, and this led to a somewhat confused supply situation. This was compounded by incompatible communications systems and this created issues with command and control. While the United States had a relatively easy victory over their opposition, the JCS official history on Operation Urgent Fury draws attention to a number of potentially very serious issues:

> Proper command and control of a joint task force with land, sea, and air components requires a truly joint headquarters. Within USLANTCOM, the Headquarters, US Forces Caribbean, provided a staff of officers from all services. However, USFORCARIB was located at Key West, Florida, a considerable distance from USLANTCOM headquarters, Norfolk, Virginia. To save time in coordinating and to maintain tight operational security, ADM McDonald chose instead Second Fleet headquarters as the 67 headquarters for the CJTF 120. Collocated with ADM McDonald's headquarters in Norfolk, Second Fleet had operational forces at its disposal; USFORCARIB was only a headquarters. USCINCLANT did add Army officers to Second Fleet headquarters during the last two days of the planning, but in the opinion of the Joint Staff, the new headquarters still lacked needed ground and air expertise.

USS *Manitowoc*, one of two LSTs accompanying USS *Guam* during Operation Urgent Fury. (US DoD)

Hence, the first few days of URGENT FURY saw uncoordinated ground operations by Rangers and Marines and the absence of unified air support.

Lack of interoperable communications exacerbated systemic lack of command and control. Here again short planning time and excessive security were contributory factors. Faced with the sudden transformation of a noncombatant evacuation operation into a joint combat operation, communications planners hurriedly made adjustments in their systems, but ran out of time before they could supply the same Communications Electronics Operating Instructions (CEOI), codes, and communications security procedures to all the combatants. Critically, communications planners were unable to provide tactical forces with compatible communications equipment. Navy radios could not communicate with the Vinson secure radio equipment used by the Army units, delaying and complicating requests for naval air and naval gunfire support. Soldiers in sight of warships delayed operations until distant Air Force gunships and Army helicopters could be summoned.

The pre-D-Day exclusion of several types of planners impeded the operation's logistical flow, civil-military relations, and public affairs. Inadequate logistics planning delayed arrival of troops, supplies, and fuel on Grenada after D-Day. To compensate, troops took needed items from local businesses or homes. Shortage of medical personnel and confusion over Medevac procedures sometimes held up treatment of the injured. Army helicopter pilots carrying wounded men had to learn the techniques for landing on naval vessels. Lack of civil affairs and public health personnel meant that combat troops had to be diverted to perform these tasks. During the early stages of URGENT FURY, PSYOPS units were not on hand to urge Grenadian cooperation with US forces. Public affairs planners in the Pentagon did not have time to organize a pool of reporters to cover the Rangers and Marines on D-day. Lack of such coverage created ill will among the US media who complained about suppression of the public right to know.[12]

Many of these lessons would prove to be crucial for the next big operation undertaken by the United States – Operation Desert Storm – in 1990. Perhaps it is no coincidence that Norman Schwarzkopf, then a Major General, served as Admiral Metcalf's ground forces advisor. In respect of logistics and public affairs, lessons were learned.

The dearth of suitable air bases was to prove a challenge for the transport of the 82nd Airborne Division. While the C-130s transporting them could land at Point Salines, with only 5,000 feet of runaway completed, only one C-141 could land at any time, with the runway at the inadequate Pearls Airport being much too short. This meant that the induction of troops and their equipment was slower than might otherwise be desirable. Many C-130s and the C-141s, not to mention the huge C-5 Galaxies, made much use of Grantley Adams International Airport as a staging area for operations.

US Force Levels – Overkill?

In the aftermath of Operation Urgent Fury, there has been some degree of criticism levelled at the United States for the quantum of force deployed to Grenada. US forces completely outnumbered their opposition. Besides being sensible, US force levels were dictated by their perception of likely opposition. The Americans committed about seven battalions of troops with air support, artillery and some armour. Against this, they assessed (wrongly) that they faced:

> There were 701 Cuban Revolutionary Armed Forces (FAR) troops on Grenada. Of these, 43 advised (and, in some cases, commanded) PRA units. Ten Ministry of Interior officers provided similar advice to the People's Revolutionary Militia (PRM). The Cuban construction engineer battalion was armed and organized as a military unit. The engineers lived in barracks, carried weapons and had received defense orders from Fidel Castro and their commander, Colonel Pedro Tortoló Comas. Air reinforcement from Cuba was possible.
>
> The Grenadian PRA was composed of two infantry battalions, an antiaircraft battery and an artillery battery. This force had trained to deal with US airborne and amphibious tactics. Its armament included six BTR60PBs and some BRDM2 armored vehicles (which are still used by the Soviets), seven 130mm towed artillery pieces and six twin 23mm towed air defense guns. The

PRA was supplemented by seven PRM infantry battalions which had conducted major anti-invasion maneuvers in April 1983.[13]

However, despite subsequent attempts at force level inflation, it is evident that the United States either deliberately inflated the force levels of its opposition, to justify its intervention and to portray Grenada as some sort of major 'threat' to US interests, or it was completely clueless as to the situation in Grenada. In the absence of information, rumours abounded.

Intelligence Gaps

The United States planning was plagued by a dearth of information and this resulted in many rumours being spread about actual conditions in Grenada. Rioting was reported on 21 October when the curfew was briefly lifted to allow residents to purchase food. More trouble was expected as the days wore on but there were increasingly erratic and exaggerated reports. These began to part company with reality. While the situation in Grenada was far from either stable or peaceful, there was no repeat of the mass killings or large-scale violence of 19 October or its subsequent days. Yet, US intelligence reports began to get more alarmist. As the JCS official history notes:

> Early in the evening of 23 October, intelligence indicated growing preparation by the Grenadian junta to mobilize popular resistance to a foreign invasion. Perhaps the news leaks about the diversion of the *Independence* battle group and MARG 1-84 had sounded the tocsin. From Barbados, the US defense attaché reported that Grenadian security guards and troops at the Richmond Hill Prison, St. George's, had received orders to kill all prisoners in the event of invasion. DIA also had unconfirmed information that British subjects and other foreign businessmen had already been executed. Meanwhile, the Barbadian National Radio spoke of growing dissatisfaction with the Grenadian armed forces over the brutal excesses of the regime and of the failure of militia members to report to their assigned units.[14]

This dearth of reliable intelligence or any form of reliable information emanating from Grenada brought to the fore the need for local assistance. As there were few US assets in Grenada, and certainly very poor means of establishing any form of contact with the students who might have provided much useful information, the United States took the step of reaching out to the Caribbean islands of Barbados and Jamaica which had the ability to get information. Particularly valuable was the role of the Barbados Defence Force which, despite being very small, took an active role in the planning and preparation of the plans for certain aspects of Operation Urgent Fury. More importantly, the BDF was able to provide vital information on the situation in Grenada. Far beyond its military potential, the BDF performed invaluable service in respect of gathering human intelligence, conducting aerial and maritime reconnaissance as well as assisting the United States with knowledge in respect of coastlines, tides and other issues of geographical importance. This assistance was to prove to be most useful to the Americans.

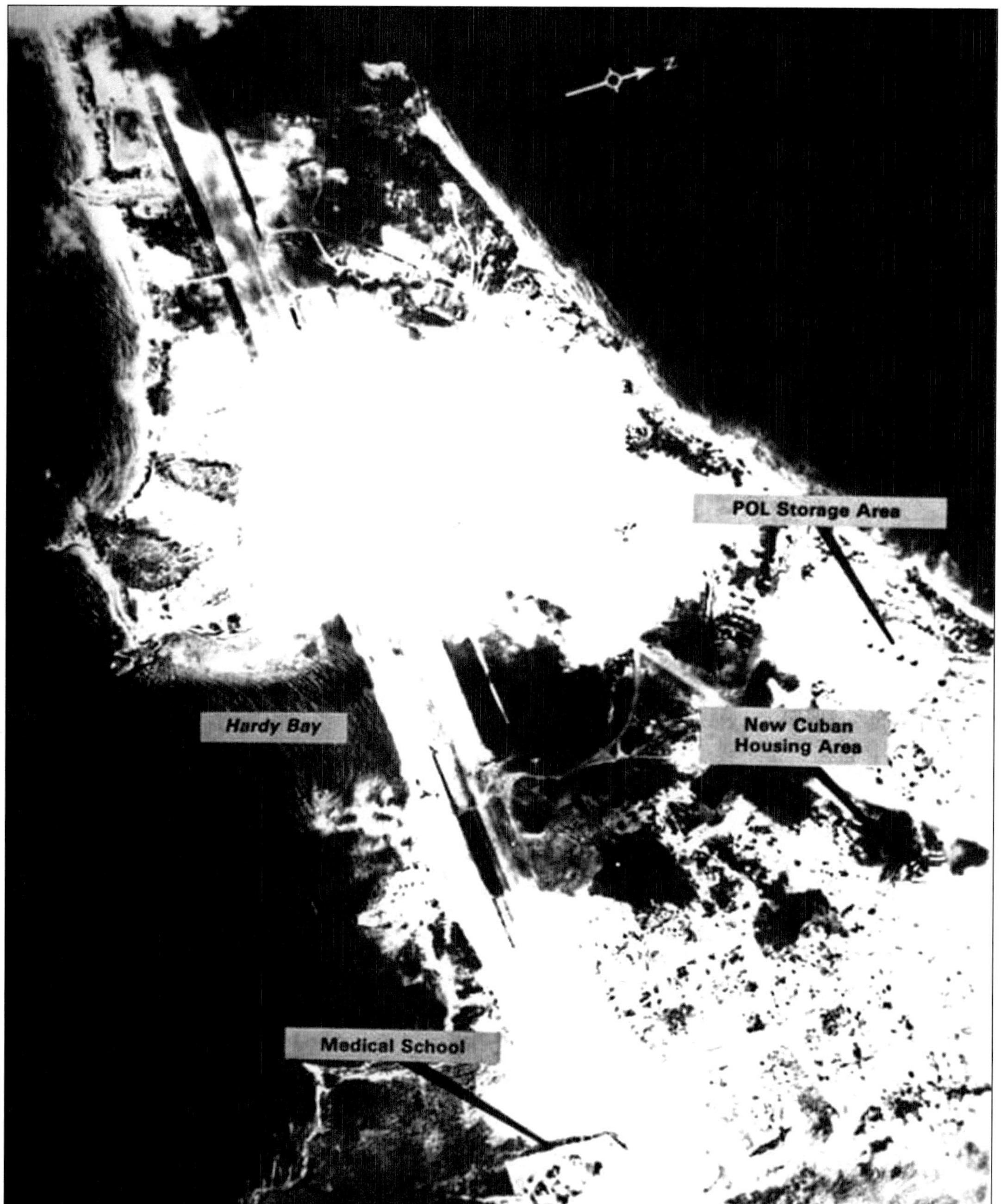

Probably taken by either a Lockheed U-2 or SR-71, this reconnaissance photograph of Point Salines Airport shows the primary objectives around it. (US DoD)

Urgent Fury – The BDF's Role

Though the Barbados Defence Force would only supply a single rifle platoon – which was deployed alongside a substantial contingent from the RBPF – to the Caribbean Peacekeeping Force in Grenada, its role was in planning the military intervention of 1983 and in so doing, it assisted considerably in Operation Urgent Fury. It should be noted that the main role arrogated onto itself by Barbados was that of planning and providing intelligence. Barbados was never under any illusion as to its military capacity to carry out any meaningful military operation against Grenada in 1983.

On 16 October 1983, Major Mark Adkin, a former British Army officer, was serving as staff officer of training and operations of the BDF. He was summoned to the office of Colonel Rudyard Lewis, the Chief of Staff of the BDF, and told to put together the outline of a plan to rescue Maurice Bishop, then still alive but being held captive by the Revolutionary Military Council now ruling Grenada. Adkin was told to make an assessment of what troops and assets might be required to rescue Bishop from house arrest, being further told that he should not concern himself with where the troops and equipment would come from, which was the first inkling that the United States was preparing a military operation into Grenada.[15]

To aid him in his task, Adkin was fortunate to have knowledge of Lieutenant Commander Peter Tomlin, who was the intelligence officer of the newly formed Regional Security System. Tomlin was an able naval officer and had a good knowledge of Grenada and of Maurice Bishop with whom he was personally acquainted, meeting the latter on several occasions including 14 March 1979, the day after Bishop's successful coup.[16] After the events of October 1979, and Bishop's overthrow and imprisonment, Tomlin captained a Barbados Coast Guard vessel into Grenada's St. George's harbour, accompanied by a CIA operative and a Canadian representative to make an assessment of the ground situation and to explore the situation of foreign nationals who might want to escape from Grenada, a circumstance deemed likely owning to the extreme tension in the country and the prospect of significant violence. The spectre of the latter was to manifest itself less than a week later when violence erupted with tragic consequences for Bishop and several members of his Cabinet along with many Grenadian civilians.

The professional skills of Adkin, and the knowledge of and reconnaissance undertaken by Tomlin was augmented by the detailed knowledge of Grenada by Major Mike Hartland, a former British Army officer who was serving with the Barbados Defence Force. Hartland had spent 11 years in Grenada, between 1968 and 1979, and knew the country as well as the key personalities involved in the ongoing crisis. The three of these officers, along with the rest of their staff, were able to create a draft plan for Bishop's rescue within a few hours of getting their instructions from Colonel Lewis.[17] This speaks volumes in respect of the professionalism of the BDF staff officers and to the value of intimate local knowledge by people familiar with the countries in question.

This plan envisaged an operation by surprise *coup de main* and anticipated a hostile reception from the Grenadian People's Revolutionary Army (PRA). The first phase would be undertaken in darkness with troops staging a heliborne assault with the principal targets being Bishop's house, where he was being held under house arrest, the Governor General's residence, the airfields and Pearls and Salines, the radio station and the stationing of troops at a number of blocking or ambush positions to the north and south of Grenadian capital, St George's. The plan did not envisage engaging or attacking PRA troop concentrations but rather preventing them from intervening while Bishop was rescued. Adkin proposed that operation would require two battalions with a third being available for deployment in the event of necessity.[18] As a rescue mission, the plan was quite realistic and it might have been quite feasible had it been approved.

The plan was received and the concept approved by Colonel Lewis who took it to Prime Minister Tom Adams but it got no further than a draft plan and no serious work was done to take the operation forward or to work towards preparing a breakdown of the force composition required to undertake this rescue mission.[19] However, Colonel Lewis and Prime Minister Adams wanted the BDF to continue to gather information and to this end, the BDF was to play a most important role in the planning for Urgent Fury, with BDF personnel and equipment being deployed in an innovative manner to maximise intelligence gathering without sophisticated surveillance equipment.

On or about 17 October, two days before Bishop's murder and the establishment of the Revolutionary Military Council, two BDF personnel – Second Lieutenant Alvin Quintyne and Lance Corporal Martia Browne – masqueraded as a couple on vacation and volunteered to covertly infiltrate Grenada to examine the situation and report on visible troop deployments. The two BDF soldiers, routing through St. Vincent, were interrogated by officials at Pearls Airport.[20] Quintyne's knowledge of Grenada, which he had visited before, was thorough enough to convince the immigration officials at Pearls of their bona fides and the two conducted as thorough a reconnaissance as possible and noted no PRA units or anti-aircraft batteries at Pearls. They were given a lift by a Cuban truck driver who was armed with an assault rifle but otherwise noted nothing particularly untoward. However, they could not reach Salines airfield but noticed many military vehicles at Frequente. Their mission was curtailed when they discovered a man attempting to look through the door of their room.[21] Quintyne decided that the two should leave and they departed on 18 October, just one day before Grenada's descent into bloody violence which led to the beginning of the end of the Grenada Revolution and the subsequent military intervention by the United States to restore what was quaintly termed 'constitutional authority' on the island.

The single aircraft of the BDF Air Wing – the lone Cessna 402C – also played its part when, on the afternoon after Bishop's murder, Lieutenant Commander Tomlin and Major Robin Keaney, recently retired from the Royal Air Force, conducted an aerial survey of Grenada where they noted little by way of military activity save for the arrival of an An-26 transport at Pearls airfield and that the runway at Salines was blocked, with all construction work on the new airport being stopped. They noted no deployment of anti-aircraft batteries and were not challenged during their flight.[22]

While the BDF Air Wing was playing its small part, Commander Roger Porteous, a Royal Navy officer on secondment to the Barbados Coast Guard and the Regional Security System, was compiling a comprehensive report on all the beaches and bays along Grenada's coastline with a view to identifying potential areas suitable for amphibious landings. He recommended the Grand Anse and Grand Mal bays on the west coast of Grenada.[23] This was to prove invaluable to the planning of the 22nd Marine Amphibious Unit which was to eventually land troops and armour at Grand Mal on 25 October 1983. The lack of knowledge of Grenada, its coast and its geography was to become one of the major issues that plagued the planning of Operation Urgent Fury.

The RSS and BDF also provided critical intelligence to the United States with the CIA representative in Barbados posing some 18 questions to the two agencies. The shocking realisation came that the CIA had no inkling of who among the People's Revolutionary Government still remained loyal to Bishop, who was in effective command of the PRA or within the Cabinet were actively supporting Bernard Coard. Worst of all, US intelligence had no accurate knowledge as to the location of the several hundred American students attending university at Grenada-based campuses. In these areas, the RSS and BDF provided much needed assistance.[24]

When the Caribbean Peace Keeping Force was established, Colonel Rudyard Lewis was promoted to Brigadier General given the role of regional coordinator, as well as being the Chief of Staff of the BDF. Actual command of the CPKF was placed in the more able and experienced hands of Colonel Ken Barnes of the Jamaica Defence Force, which contributed the single largest contingent of troops to the CPKF and were the only ones regarded as being combat capable by the Americans.[25] The BDF contributed a reinforced rifle platoon of 50 combat personnel while over 100 personnel of the RBPF, armed with an eclectic mix of 7.62mm SLRs and 0.303" Rifle No.4 Mk.1s, spearheaded a force of police personnel from OECS states. These police forces were instrumental in rebuilding the shattered Royal Grenada Police Force and in maintaining law and order on the island.

As can be seen, the BDF played an important role in the early stages of planning the intervention in Grenada, far outweighing its small actual military participation in the CPKF. The BDF staff officers, acting in concert with the RSS, was able to utilise its limited physical and human resources to provide invaluable intelligence about Grenada and the disposition of PRA troops and, more importantly, their state of apparent readiness. The plan for a rescue operation to free Prime Minister Bishop might, had it been executed promptly, have worked had the plan been taken more seriously but that should not detract from the excellent performance of the BDF.

The RMC Defence Plans

In the days of the PRG, Bishop foresaw a possibility that a CIA-supported group of Grenadian exiles or mercenaries would attempt to stage a Bay of Pigs-type of invasion, supported by some heavy equipment and maybe light attack aircraft. To this end, defence plans based around a holding action by the PRA against an amphibious landing were prepared. The PRA was to contain any invasion force that it could not easily repel. Thereafter the PRM would be rapidly mobilised to swarm the invading force with moderately trained but adequately armed personnel.[26]

In early 1983, prior to Bishop's ousting, President Ronald Reagan's criticism of the expansion of the Point Salines Airport and Cuba's involvement, the PRG revamped its defence plans to include the defence of Point Salines and its peninsula. The General Staff and Cuban military advisors laid out an elaborate defence plan based around mortars and light machine guns with interlocking fields of fire, with the entire peninsula being defended from pre-determined fighting positions. Cuban construction workers, all of whom had served as conscripts, would be tasked with this but their training as a unit had not begun by October 1983.[27]

As an inevitable conflict loomed after 19 October 1983, the RMC found itself with fewer resources and a more unwilling ally than the PRG plans had envisaged. With the vast majority of the PRM not responsive, as has been shown, the PRAF was able to muster well under 800 personnel and of these, some were of dubious value. The PRAF realised that its headquarters and the supply depot at Frequente were vulnerable to air attack. They also were quite accurate in determining the main area of US operations – the southwest and St. George's with Point Salines and the beach and Grand Anse being prime objectives.[28]

To deal with the vulnerability of its headquarters and the depots at Frequente, Second Lieutenant Fraser was tasked with shifting the stores to another location. Despite lacking adequate transport, Fraser was able to move some reserve stocks to the Good Hope Estate in the hills four kilometres east of St. George's.[29] An alternative command post was selected at The Park, on the slopes of Mount Pleasant but in the event, this was never used. A shortage of manpower, however, precluded the defence of anything other than the southwest; even Pearls Airport was left completely undefended, though its control tower was within range of PRM guns tasked with its destruction.

The RMC plans envisaged having some four infantry companies of approximately 100 men each, three of which were regular PRA and the other from the PRM. It also supposedly mobilised two batteries of six ZU-23-2s apiece – one each from the PRA and the PRM – plus two such guns attached to the mobile company at Calivigny.[30] The PRM was able to field three platoons each of two M53 quad 12.7mm machine guns for anti-aircraft duty and these were to play an important role. The PRAF lacked any early warning radar and its anti-aircraft weapons were all optically sighted and without passive night-vision equipment.

The motorised rifle company was placed under the command of Second Lieutenant Nelson who also took control of the mobile company as its commander (Officer Cadet Mayers) had been killed in the events of 19 October. Nelson thus had nearly half of the effective strength of the PRA at his disposal though he was a very junior officer. In the motorised company, two platoons were mounted in BTR-60 APCs with the third in GAZ trucks.

The company had seven BTRs on strength (the eighth having broken down at Frequente). The motorised company also had an anti-tank unit with two ageing 75mm recoilless rifles.[31] These weapons were of little use against modern main battle tanks of the early 1980s but could be very effective against APCs, light armour and devastating against soft-skin vehicles such as trucks and jeeps. The PRA's anti-tank crews were not particularly well-trained and had no experience of engaging any sort of armour. They would not know the vulnerable points of the USMC's M60A1 tanks nor the appropriate ranges and angles at which they could engage such vehicles.

Augmenting the motorised company, under Nelson's overall command, was the mobile company of three rifle platoons mounted on GAZ trucks. All platoons were led by sergeants except the attached mortar platoon with three 82mm mortars which was led by a warrant officer. The anti-aircraft platoon with its two ZU-23-2 guns was led by a sergeant. The two companies, combined into a small infantry battle group, all regular PRA soldiers, was the main striking force of the PRA and was a reasonably balanced outfit, that was mobile and adequately trained, albeit very small and lacking artillery support or modern anti-tank weapons. They were tasked with defending St. George's. Nelson settled his forces in the concentration area at Mount Parnassus, two kilometres east of St. George's with the motorised company having moved out from Fort Frederick and the mobile company having moved out of Calivigny to concentrate at their new location.[32]

The PRM proved, as noted earlier, to be the undoing of all the PRAF's defence plans. Of its notional strength of 2,000 to 3,000, only 257 showed up for duty and the two battalions available to Region I managed to field a total of 120 personnel between them. The security company of the PRA, stretched by its commitments to breaking point, was reinforced with 50 of these personnel. The remaining 70 were placed under the command of Lieutenant Iman Abdullah and, constituting the rapid mobilisation company, was given the impossible task of defending Grand Anse with only rifles and light machine guns for firepower and little transport to cover the distance from Ross Point in the north to Quarantine Point in the south.[33]

The third company of PRA regulars was the security company which was tasked with static guard duties and which was split into detachments of no larger than 20 personnel and tasked with the defence of Fort Rupert, Fort Frederick, Mount Weldale, the Richmond Hill Prison, the depots at Frequente and a few token guards at the university campuses at True Blue and Grand Anse.[34] In addition, a single squad was tasked with providing routine security at Point Salines but not with its defence which was left to the Cuban construction workers – a decision which would have fateful consequences thanks to the extremely restrictive rules of engagement imposed on the Cubans from their leadership, both political and military.

Cuban Rules of Engagement – Crippling the RMC

Bernard Coard was a supremely pragmatic individual and realised that the best chance that the RMC had of surviving any US intervention and warding off its inevitable oblivion, was through the use of the Cuban construction workers and Cuban assistance. General Hudson Austin wanted Cuban construction workers formed into combat units and placed under Grenadian command while simultaneously requesting reinforcements of troops from Cuba. Cuba refused to oblige him in respect of either request. As has been discussed, the friendship between Castro and Bishop and the latter's murder left the Cuban leader displeased.

Cuba's options were very limited, even if they had wished to assist the RMC. The United States would not allow Cuban transports to bring in any significant number of Cuban troops to reinforce the PRA, and Cuba's own transport aviation assets were incapable of transporting any heavy equipment such as armour or artillery. Despite Coard being known to be close to the USSR, the latter had no assets in the region nor did it appear to have any discernible desire to assist the RMC in any practical way. The real question for the RMC was whether Cuba would assist them.

Castro answered the RMC's request for help with a rather terse series of communications in which he harangued the RMC for its murder of Bishop, the death of civilians and for the subsequent loss of popular support for the RMC. He made clear that his desire was for the RMC to reconcile with the Grenadian people, identify those responsible for the murder of Bishop and punish them appropriately. This was, of course, not to the liking of any of the RMC's members. However, they were in accord with Castro's admonition that they should not interfere with any evacuation of civilians.[35]

In response to their request for troops, however, two of Castro's messages sealed the fate of the RMC:

> If the US intervenes, we must vigorously defend ourselves as if we were in Cuba, in our camp sites, in our workplaces close by, but only if we are directly attack. I repeat: only if we are directly attacked. We would thus be defending ourselves, not the Government or its deeds. If the Yankees land on the runway section near the University or on its surroundings to evacuate its citizens, fully refrain from interfering [...] our force, essential made up of civilian cooperation workers, is too small to be considered as a significant military factor vis-à-vis a large scale US invasion [...] sending reinforcements is impossible and unthinkable.
>
> Cuban personnel will defend their positions, that is the runway up to the Hardy Bay filling and the area between Point Salines and Morne Rouge [...] It would be better that area [referring here to the True Blue Campus] were free of military personnel so that it would not be regarded as a battle ground which could justify armed actions by imperialism under the pretext of evacuating its citizens.[36]

These instructions were further compounded by communications problems between Havana and the Cuban construction workers at Point Salines. It is debatable whether Castro intended the Cubans to take up defensive positions or operate proactively to secure Point Salines. They, however, interpreted their instructions to mean that they should remain in their camps with weapons kept in barracks. This inevitably meant that they were neither deployed nor prepared for combat. They were unable to deploy to their pre-determined fighting positions and this left the central and eastern portions of the runaway undefended.

Furthermore, the Cubans refused to allow the PRA to enter their assigned zone, thus completely undermining the defence of Point Salines.[37] This was to prove catastrophic during the landing operations at Point Salines when the Cubans chose not to initiate hostilities against US forces, thus allowing them to escape relatively unscathed at a time when they were most vulnerable. Moreover, the Cubans did not conduct any joint planning or training with the PRAF in the days leading up to Urgent Fury thus ensuring no coordination between the defending forces and very poor communication.

By choosing to effectively confine themselves to their barracks, and in the absence of any reinforcements from Cuba, the Cuban construction workers abandoned the PRAF to its fate. Some of the Cuban military advisors were more proactive and aided the PRA and PRM in directing their anti-aircraft guns and in preparing and planning defensive operations. However, for all practical purposes, Castro's Cubans had left the RMC to its fate. Unfortunately, even these rules of engagement placed Cubans in harm's way.

The RMC Waits

The RMC could hardly be faulted for their threat appreciation or the priorities that governed its deployment. However, thanks to its own actions and brutality, it ensured that it lacked the forces to make its dispositions sufficiently strong to offer any sort of viable defence against an attack. This led to a degree of unreality with tiny units being assigned defensive tasks for which they would be hopelessly inadequate and for which they lacked sufficient resources.

As indicated above, Point Salines was to be left to the Cubans whose instructions were merely to defend their work areas if fired upon. This meant that the Bishop-era plan of early 1983 with its pre-designated defensive position and interlocking fields of fire from mortars and machine guns collapsed completely. Even worse, the RMC had hoped to station the PRM ZU-23-2 battery with its six guns at Point Salines but this too came to nought as the PRM gun crews failed to report for duty, once again reflecting the lack of support for the RMC.[38]

The rest of the anti-aircraft defences were somewhat more fortunate with the PRA ZU-23-2 battery being tasked with the defence of St. George's minus a two-gun platoon which was assigned to the logistics base at Frequente. Of the remaining four guns, two were deployed at Fort Rupert and two at Fort Frederick. Four M53 quad 12.7mm guns were deployed to St. George's to support the

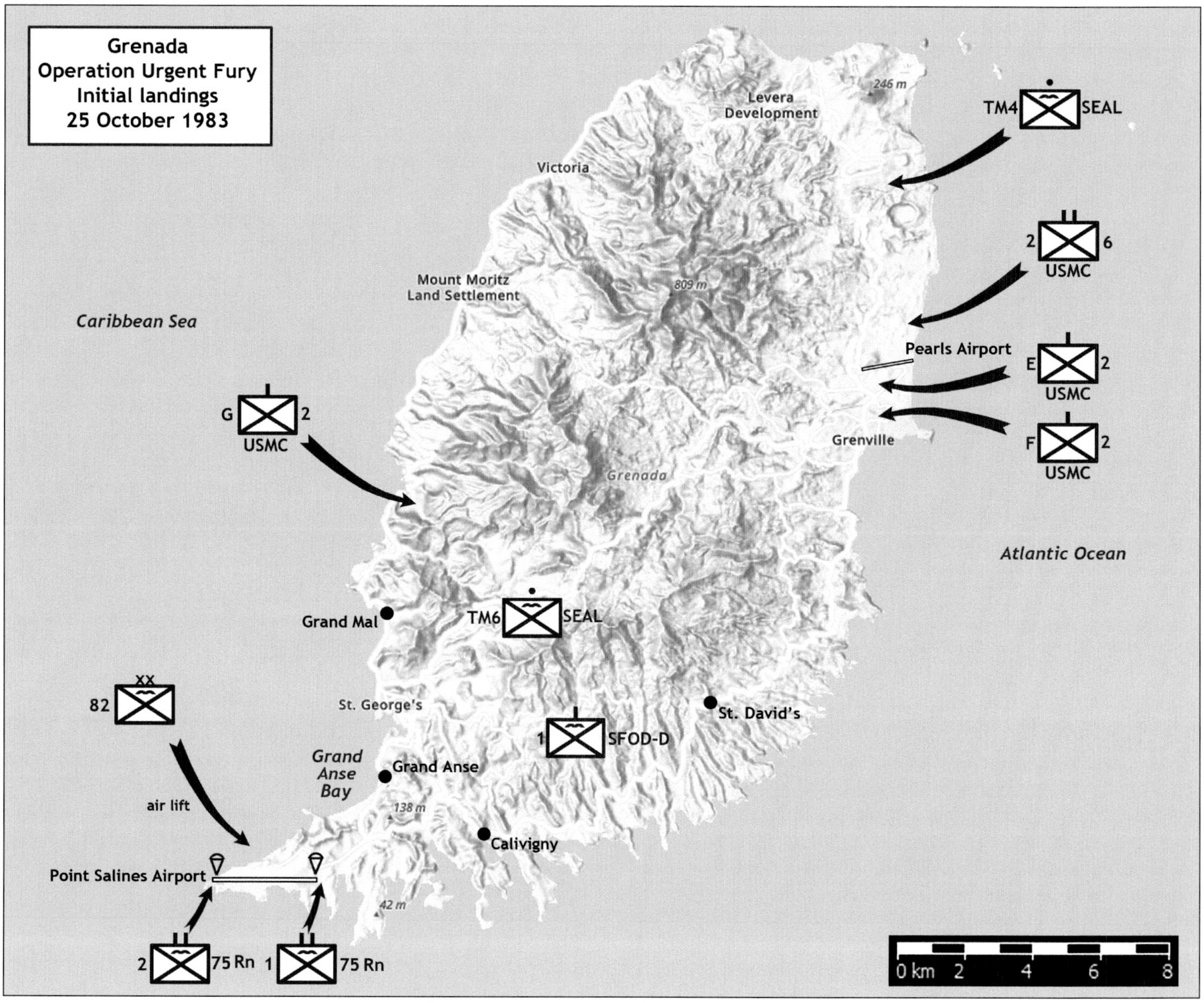

A map showing initial landings of the US Forces. (USMC)

23mm guns and two more were deployed at D'Arbeau above the quarry east of Queen's Park. The guns at D'Arbeau were dug-in and tased with protecting both the Mount Weldale and the nearby power station. It should be noted that though these M53 guns had PRM crews, they were professionally handled.[39]

Pearls Airport was left bereft of PRA personnel – none being available – and it was envisaged that the PRM from Region II would undertake this task with a delaying action being contemplated. Two more M53 12.7mm guns were positioned on the hill north of the runway. These were tasked with destroying the control tower if it looked as if it would fall to American troops. Finally, the RMC leadership moved into the tunnels under Fort Rupert, safe from air attack but out of radio communications with their field units.[40]

In some ways, while their actions of 19 October 1983 can never be condoned, one may find a certain level of respect for the PRA and even the RMC leadership. Forsaken by their allies, outmatched in every respect and isolated from their own people by their own conduct, they chose to prepare and plan their defences, knowing the end was nigh. RMC and PRAF planning was, in the circumstances, relatively realistic and made good use of the few resources at their disposal. Of particular note, however, is the RMC leadership isolating itself from communication with its forces and leaving leadership to junior officers. As the hours ticked down to US intervention, the PRAF had no idea of when it would come, only that it would come.

It came on 25 October with the Marines launching from the USS *Guam* at 0315 hours.

6
URGENT FURY

Day One, 25 October 1983: The Marines Land

Though the first Marine CH-46 launched from the USS *Guam* at 0315 hours, a combination of factors required the aircraft to launch, assemble in formation, land again to pick up their assigned troops and then top-up their fuel. It took until 0500 hours to get all 21 helicopters on their way to Grenada which was only 16 kilometres (10 miles) away. They were assigned to LZ Buzzard, under one kilometre away from Pearls Airport. The first Marines touched down, unopposed, at 0520 hours. They were 20 minutes behind schedule but were still ahead of other US troops.[1]

While the first Marines were not engaged, the two 12.7mm M53s on the hill near Pearls opened fire on the subsequent helicopters. The PRM gunners were able to use the breaking dawn to illuminate the helicopters and for a brief period of time, the transport helicopters were taken under heavy fire from the quadruple heavy machine gun mounts. However, while the Marines were surprised, escorting USMC AH-1T Sea Cobra helicopters quickly neutralised the guns with a combination of 20mm gunfire and rockets.[2] It should be noted that despite being put out of action early, the PRM crews stood by their weapons bravely and escaped the return fire from the helicopters. They were, of, course, completely ineffective in downing any of these particular helicopters but the fact that there was resistance was indicative that the Marines and other US troops might face additional problems in the future as they progressed.

The landing of the Marines, on the other hand, was disrupted out of all proportions to the light anti-aircraft fire that the PRM gunners were able to produce. The disembarkation of troops was now increasingly rushed, with helicopters landing, disembarking their Marines and taking off in under 15 seconds. One Marine broke an arm being shoved out of a helicopter. Vehicles also suffered; one jeep was pushed off and sank in marshy ground with two more becoming entangled while being unloaded from a CH-53, one Marine breaking a leg while trying to untangle these two trapped vehicles.[3] These injuries were avoidable but perhaps were only to be expected

A CH-46E Sea Knight on the deck of USS *Guam*, warming up its engines before the take-off. (US DoD)

The view forward from the island of USS *Guam*, showing another two CH-46s preparing for take-off at the start of Operation Urgent Fury. (US DoD, via Albert Grandolini)

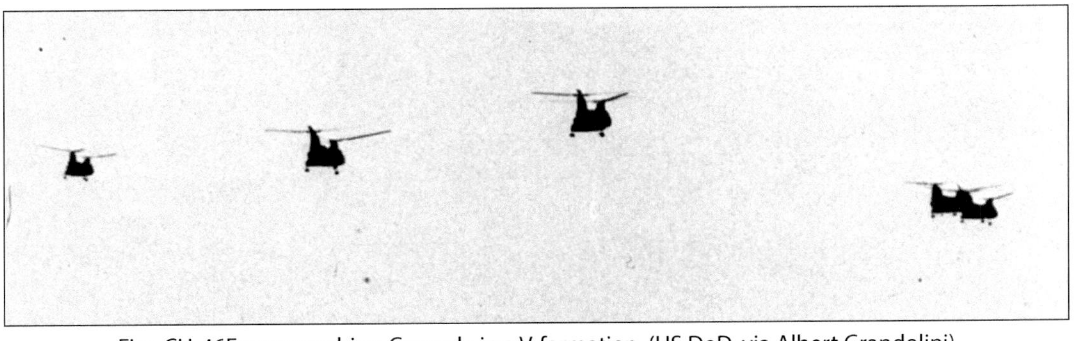

Five CH-46Es approaching Grenada in a V-formation. (US DoD, via Albert Grandolini)

An AH-1T of the US Marines flying low over Grenada, early on 25 October 1983. Note the 20mm gun in the chin turret under the front cockpit, and a total of four launchers for 68mm HYDRA unguided rockets. Each MAU usually had four AH-1Ts embarked on its amphibious assault ships, but 22nd MAU was reinforced with at least two additional AH-1Js for Operation Urgent Fury. (US DoD)

A CH-53D landing near a captured ZU-23-2 AA gun. (US National Archives)

An ancient An-2, donated to Bishop's PRG for crop spraying, found at Pearls Airport. (US National Archives)

in the somewhat confusing environment into which the Marines found themselves and the lack of knowledge about the island.

Two platoons of Echo Company from the 2nd Battalion/8th Marines, 22nd MAU moved to secure the hill from which the M53s had fired. The PRM crews, who had taken cover, had returned to their weapons but did not fire on the advancing Marines. The crews fled at this point. Echo company secured Pearls Airport which was by now in a dilapidated state and capable of only facilitating turboprop transports with the facility lacking landing lights and modern electronic navigational aids. In bad weather, Pearls had to be closed down as being incapable of handling any commercial traffic.[4] However, this was a major success for the Americans as, without any major fighting, they had captured a useful airfield onto which they could resupply their forces on the island.

On the airfield, however, the Marines took possession of the only two aircraft available, at least potentially, to the RMC. One was an AN-26, which had transported Colonel Tortoló and which was wearing the livery of Cubana Airlines. There was no indication that this aircraft was militarised in any way. On the other hand, an ancient AN-2 biplane transport, still in the markings of AEROFLOT, which had been donated to Bishop's PRG for crop-spraying, was found with parachute-rigging equipment in its cabin. Neither aircraft had played any role in the military operations though the 12-man crew of the AN-26 was taken into custody, making them the first Cuban prisoners of the conflict though none of them were combatants and none were armed.[5]

The fighting at Pearls officially marked the start of hostilities between the RMC and the United States. Fortunately, despite the injuries sustained by a few Marines during their hasty disembarkation, there were no casualties caused by hostile action on either side. It should also be noted that at this time, the Marines had not encountered either PRA regulars or the anticipated Cuban troops. There was no PRA or Cuban presence at Pearls or in most of the areas where the 400 Marines landed during that first day. With the tiny PRM forces at Pearls now dispersed, the US Marines were able to declare Pearls Airport secured by 0730 on 25 October 1983.

Fox Company of the 8th Battalion, 22nd MAU, landed at the port town of Grenville where their reception could not have been more different. The helicopters landed in a football field and the US troops noticed that civilians were waving to them in welcome. At this point, the Lieutenant Colonel Grenville Amos decided to adopt a different approach and chose to tread carefully as the population was not hostile, helping the Marines to identify PRM and PRA personnel who had discarded their uniforms and returned to civilian life plus loaning the Marines vehicles. The 400 Marines who landed quickly learned that the level of resistance depended upon the level of ideological commitment that the PRA and PRM troops had to the new RMC. Most, as it turned out, had next to no loyalty to the new regime and reacted accordingly.[6]

However, with little resistance and no combat casualties, the Marines had captured both Pearls Airport and the port of Grenville. This meant that the US forces could bring in additional reinforcements by air and sea without significant challenges from hostile forces. A far more serious issue was the extremely limited capacity of both installations. This was particularly the case with Pearls where larger US transport aircraft would have considerable difficulty in landing, much less unloading, high-volume cargoes. Point Salines was a much more important target and despite the Cubans having blocked the runway, the US forces assigned to it needed to secure that objective.

The RMC had by this time begun using Radio Free Grenada to call frantically for the PRM to mobilise and for citizens to resist the invasion.

Neither happened.

They also called for their foreign 'allies' to help them.

They got none.

The Rangers Take Point Salines

Sometime before the Marines landed, a number of people, including Major Einstein Louison in his cell at the Richmond Hill Prison, heard sounds of at least one aircraft flying over St George's at between 0300 hours and 0430 hours on 25 October 1983. This was a reconnaissance AC-130 Spectre gunship flown by Major Michael Couvillon with the pathfinder group of the Rangers who were about to begin the US invasion of Grenada. The pathfinders were to do a free-fall drop over Salines and report on the ground situation to the rest of A Company 1st/75th Rangers. They would seek to identify and mark with lights either the landing zone or drop zone. The main body of A Company would travel in two MC-130s with five more C-130s bringing in the rest of 1st/75th Rangers who would drop into the area or land, depending on the circumstances.[7]

The Rangers had the task of securing the airfield east of Hardy Bay and, perhaps much more importantly, securing the US citizens at the medical college at True Blue. It was not clear whether a drop or a landing would be needed but the Rangers do not seem to have anticipated any serious opposition and had prepared the loading of the aircraft expecting that they would be landing.[8]

The 1st/75th Rangers were to be followed by the 2nd/75th Rangers. This battalion was to land and to secure the runway west of Hardy Bay, regroup and march quickly to Calivigny. The two Ranger battalions would have air support from three AC-130s on call and the whole operation in the south of Grenada would be controlled from an EC-130 with Major General Richard Scholtes aboard. Once the airfield at Point Salines was secured, he would set up his command post at the site and by 1200 hours, he was expecting the 82nd Airborne Division who would take over from the two Ranger battalions.[9]

This plan was fairly radically changed, with the Rangers departing much earlier to allow the pathfinders adequate time on the ground. They got news that an attempted reconnaissance effort by the SEALs had failed with four parachute fatalities. At about 0330 hours, the pathfinder team prepared to jump. Almost immediately things went bad. Not only did the AC-130 attract anti-aircraft fire from the PRAF depot at Frequente, but two of the pathfinders fell to their deaths when something went wrong with either their parachutes or their altimeters. It was a decidedly inauspicious start to the Ranger operation.[10]

By 0400 hours, the Rangers learned that the runway at Point Salines had been blocked by the Cubans. At this point, Lieutenant Colonel Wesley Taylor made the decision that everybody in the 1st/75th Rangers, minus administrative personnel and crews for the machine-gun armed jeeps, would jump. This created some confusion as Taylor's instructions were misunderstood and chaos reigned as

Taylor's men of 1st/75th Rangers descending under their parachutes upon Point Salines Airport. (US DoD)

A ZU-23-2 AA gun, the same type that fired from Frequente. This example captured on Grenada was photographed immediately after the US intervention and is shown with its barrels elevated near vertically. (US National Archives)

Deck crew of USS *Guam* evacuating a casualty from an MH-6A Little Bird of TF 160 on 25 October 1983. (US DoD)

An M53 quad 12.7mm AA gun captured at Frequente, towed by a Land Rover. (US National Archives)

the troops sought to rig their equipment and themselves for a drop. Even then, on at least three C-130s, the orders came too late and as such three of the aircraft had to orbit Point Salines while the rest of the 1st/75th Rangers jumped. At 0531 hours, Taylor led his men into action. It was an example of how not to conduct a jump but it was no fault of Taylor's or the other Rangers.[11]

At Point Salines, the Cubans were confined to their barracks and to their mission headquarters, 'Little Havana'. Colonel Tortoló and Carlos Andres Diaz Larranga, of the Cuban Communist Party, were at Little Havana. It was at Point Salines and nearby Little Havana, and only at these locations, that Cubans and Americans were to clash. Though armed and having

A C-141 Starlifter of the US Air Force at Point Salines, around 1400hrs of 25 October 1983. (Albert Grandolini Collection)

Rangers of the 2nd Platoon 1st/75th Rangers being briefed for their next mission. Note the M151 jeep armed with an M60 machine gun and fitted with a night vision device. (US National Archives)

US Army Rangers with assault rifles and a machine gun captured at Point Salines. (US National Archives)

gone through military training, the 636 Cuban construction workers were ageing – the average age was 38 with many over 50 – and unfit. Even the 43 Cuban military advisors had only six infantry instructors among them. It was a very uneven fight, made worse by the extremely restrictive orders given to the Cubans from Havana. They had rifles and about 100 rounds per man, some SPG-9s and mortars. However, they were not to initiate combat against the Americans.[12]

Lieutenant Colonel Orlando Matamoros Lopez, who was responsible for the defence of Little Havana, and the rest of the Cuban mission were awoken by the sound of anti-aircraft fire from Frequente. Arming himself, he clearly saw the Rangers dropping onto the runway. It was amazing, however, that despite the US planning, the operation took nearly 90 minutes to complete. Had the Cubans been given different orders, it is quite possible that the US troops landing at Point Salines might have suffered severe casualties during their drop.

The US aircraft were coming under sustained fire from the ZU-23-2 guns at Frequente while at Salines itself, the PRAF had managed to install a M53 quad 12.7mm machine gun, northwest of the runaway. These guns tried to engage the C-130s. Couvillon's AC-130 opened fire and seriously wounded Second Lieutenant Frazer of PRA, its chief logistics officer. However, aboard that AC-130, the 40mm gun refused to track while one of the 20mm guns suffered feed and ejection issues. However, the AC-130 was able to suppress the PRA guns sufficiently to allow the Rangers to secure some sort of foothold on the runway. However, the element of surprise was completely lost and there would be a brisk struggle for Point Salines which might have gone either way for the US troops.[13]

By 0534 hours, Taylor and 42 Rangers from a platoon of B Company 1st/75th Rangers were on the ground. There were adequate defensive positions and had these been occupied by the PRA, the Rangers would have been slaughtered. However, the Cubans defending Point Salines were unclear as to what to do and did not open fire. The Rangers were able, under covering fire from two AC-130s that suppressed the guns at Frequente, to clear the runway of all obstructions using a captured Cuban bulldozer. By 0730 hours, the battalion was on the ground and had begun to get itself into some degree of shape to fulfil one of their primary objectives, securing the US students at True Blue.[14]

To do this, Captain Abizaid was able to coordinate the platoons of A Company with the 1st and 3rd platoons attacking across the runway with M60 machine guns and 60mm mortars. The 2nd Platoon was to approach True Blue along the beach south of the runway. As the 1st and 3rd platoons approached the village of Calliste, they came under fire from a school, killing Private Mark Okamura Yamane. One of the squad leaders, Sergeant Manous Boles from the 1st Platoon, led an attack using a captured bulldozer.[15] They found the school abandoned along with a M53 12.7mm gun. Shortly thereafter, the Rangers were able to secure the True Blue campus after an exchange of fire with the few PRA guards on duty. The PRA retreated and no students were harmed in the brief combat.[16]

Sergeant Randy Cline of A Company was assigned the task securing a road junction about 200 metres north of the True Blue

Two of the three BTR-60PBs that attacked Point Salines. (US National Archives)

relatively few casualties on either side and soon surrender negotiations began between the two sides.

Captain Newman of B Company 1st/75th Rangers, seeking to rescue two wounded Ranger scouts who were pinned down by enemy fire, called on the Cubans to surrender in Spanish. An initial set of two surrendered with Sergeant Clayton securing the surrender of 70 more and their wounded as well as being able to destroy most of the Cubans' heavy weapons. Gradually, running out of ammunition, poorly trained as a unit and with little motivation, the Cuban construction workers either withdrew when their ammunition was exhausted or when wounded, or they surrendered.[20]

By 1000 hours on 25 October, the two Ranger battalions were firmly in control of their positions on the north of the runway. Point Salines airfield had been taken and was secure enough for the rest of the Rangers to arrive. Within four hours of the first chaotic drop, nine of the twelve C-130s bringing in the Rangers and equipment had landed and unloaded. Scholtes was able to set up his headquarters and the area was secure enough to allow TF 160 to position its UH-60s and Little Birds.[21]

With Point Salines secured, at 1405, the first C-141 Starlifter landed with troops of the 82nd Airborne Division. Major General Trobaugh arrived with the first aircraft and was greeted with the pleasant news that Cubans had begun to surrender and that, while there was some confusion, the fact was that the Rangers had managed to secure both Point Salines and the US students at True Blue with minimal casualties and had neutralised the core of the Cuban resistance on the island.[22]

However, at about 1530 hours, the PRA launched its third counter-attack of the day – the first two being at Beauséjour and the Governor General's mansion (described later). Second Lieutenant Nelson had seen his motorised company effectively cannibalised and used piecemeal with an APC being dispatched to Beauséjour and two more to the Governor General's mansion. He was left with a single platoon with three BTR-60s and 24 men. Lieutenant Colonel Layne ordered him at about 1500 hours to launch an attack against the Rangers at Point Salines. The remaining motorised platoon, commanded by Warrant Officer McEwen, was to approach Point Salines through a roundabout route through St. George's.[23] They had no idea as to the disposition of US forces, nor any idea of the

campus. In a jeep equipped with a M60 machine gun, Cline and four Rangers ended up travelling two kilometres before they realised they were in the wrong place. As they turned around, they ran into an ambush set up by the PRA's security company under Redhead. The jeep was wrecked by RPG fire and Cline and three of his crewmen – Privates Maynard, Rademacher and Robinson – were killed. One other Ranger, Private Romick was wounded but was able to walk back to his unit.[17]

B Company had been tasked with securing the control tower as well as the hills beyond the terminal. The Cubans resisted briefly but the Rangers easily overcame them with one Cuban killed and 22 captured. From the hills, they could see Little Havana as the Cubans tried to set up two mortars. Using a captured PRAF M53 gun, they were able to scatter the Cuban mortar crews.[18]

However, just west of the Cuban compound, a Cuban SPG-9 recoilless rifle was proving to be problematic for A Company. Pulling back, but leaving observation posts in position, A Company summoned assistance from gunships. Admiral Metcalf provided four AH-1T Sea Cobras to assist. Two of these helicopters engaged the Cuban gunners with 20mm cannon fire and TOW ATGMs.[19] This neutralised some of the most intense Cuban resistance with

The third of the BTR-60PBs that attacked Point Salines, after being hit by fire from a USAF AC-130H. (US National Archives)

US Army Rangers with 90mm recoilless rifles. (US National Archives)

strength of the opposition they might encounter.

Nelson, convinced of the uselessness of such a small force against an entrenched enemy, rushed off to try to stop him. He encountered Redhead and elements of the Security Company of the PRA which had been involved in the fighting at Calliste. Unfortunately for McEwen, Nelson did not succeed in catching him and the motorised platoon, the strongest remaining unit in the PRA, headed towards Point Salines to engage the Rangers.

At about 1530 hours, A Company of 1st/75th Rangers noticed that three BTR-60s were approaching fast and, having passed through the company's 2nd Platoon's position, began to open fire on the runway. The 2nd Platoon engaged them with LAW rockets but while two of the APCs might have been hit, they were not disabled and the attack pressed on towards the eastern end of the airport where two Ranger companies were located.[24]

The A companies of both the 1st/75th and the 2nd/75th Ranger battalions opened fire on the advancing APCs with all the weapons at their disposal – small arms, machine guns, LAW rockets and 90mm recoilless rifles. The lead APC was hit by a LAW which caused it to crash into the second one following close behind. With these two vehicles immobile, the Rangers proceeded to engage with 90mm recoilless rifles. The vehicles were hit and their crews abandoned them with several PRA soldiers, including the gallant Sergeant McEwan, being killed. The third APC tried to escape but an AC-130 Spectre gunship put paid to that plan when one of its 105mm howitzer rounds knocked the vehicle onto its side.[25] With this single action, the PRA had lost its last cohesive motorised infantry unit.

It was a brave, but entirely futile gesture and they were to meet a bad end for no tangible military result, though it was hoped that the APCs would be able to disable at least one US aircraft and shut down the airport. In theory, it could have worked. However, unsupported by dismounted infantry or indirect weapons fire, it was a doomed operation.

The 2nd Platoon was tasked with scouting in the aftermath of this rather ambitious counterattack with Lieutenant Sydney Farrar leading a gun-jeep reconnaissance. Passing the wrecked vehicle of Sergeant Cline, they noticed an abandoned ZU-23-2, dropped by the third APC as it made its attack. At this point, PRA survivors from the APC attack engaged the Rangers in a brisk firefight which wounded Farrar. The arrival of A-6 Intruder attack aircraft put paid to this last gesture by the PRA at Point Salines.[26]

However, this gesture against the Rangers, feeble though it might have been, caused the Americans sufficient concern to ensure that the Americans continued to build up forces on Grenada with the 82nd Airborne augmenting its strength with additional battalions and support equipment.

The Caribbean Peacekeepers Arrive: Unexpectedly

Of course, things were not without additional confusion. At 1045 hours, Lieutenant Colonel Hagler of 2nd/75th Rangers was astonished to see a C-130 disgorging what he thought were PRA troops. It was typical of the rushed planning for Operation Urgent Fury that the arrival of the CPKF was confusing, no more so than to the Caribbean troops themselves.[27]

The CPKF had no clear instructions and no idea of their specific duties. The soldiers of the JDF and BDF were prepared to fight the PRA and Cubans but were not under US command and had not been integrated into the joint planning for Urgent Fury. The CPKF had, as noted earlier, about 300 personnel.[28] These included an infantry company with a mortar detachment from Jamaica, a reinforced rifle platoon from Barbados, a 14-man squad from the tiny Antigua and Barbuda Defence Force and armed police SSU units from the police forces of Dominica, St. Lucia and St. Kitts, the latter sending five policemen, but two of those chose not to go to Grenada. The next day, a unit from St. Vincent arrived along with a large BPF contingent – the latter to prove to be invaluable in the aftermath of Urgent Fury.

Brigadier Lewis of the BDF was acutely aware of the fact that his force was not fully integrated into US planning. He then spoke with Major General George Crist of the US Marines. It was decided that

CPKF soldiers – probably from Jamaica – armed with 7.62mm SLRs. (US National Archives)

CPKF troops conferring. (US National Archives)

CPKF troops on patrol. (US National Archives)

CKPF personnel from Barbados and police SSUs preparing for deployment. (US National Archives)

Barbados Police Force personnel, armed with .303 Enfield rifles, arrive along with St. Vincent SSU personnel. (US National Archives)

CPKF personnel from a Police SSU armed with 7.62mm SLRs. (US National Archives)

CPKF troops – likely from the Jamaica Defence Force – boarding a UH-60 helicopter. (US National Archives)

the CPKF could play a useful role in guarding the ever-increasing number of prisoners. By nightfall on 25 October, there were at least 250 prisoners, including a dozen from the PRA, the rest being Cuban construction workers. Colonel Barnes of the JDF, despite his unfamiliarity with the role of being military police, set to work guarding the prisoners, with Cuban medical officers being assigned to treat the wounded while Cuban cooks provided adequate food to the prisoners. This was a task that would continue for the duration of the CPKF's participation.[29]

The CPKF would, at around 1900 hours, play a useful role in assisting the SEALs trapped in the Governor General's mansion – an operation which will be detailed later. Brigadier Lewis was able to speak to Sir Paul Scoon and reassure him. Schotles reported that the SEALs were noticing that the PRA counter-attacks were coming from the official Prime Minister's residence and across a tennis court. Major Hartland of the BDF was summoned to Schotles's headquarters where, with his extensive knowledge of Grenada, he was able to explain the layout of the Government House compound and pinpoint the tennis court. This enabled the Spectre gunships supporting the SEALs to fire with excellent results, causing the PRA to withdraw.[30]

Special Operations Forces at St. George's – Surprise Lost

Even before the Marine helicopters launched from the USS *Guam* on 25 October, US Special Operations Command of the JSOC were already on the ground in Grenada, though not yet engaged. TF 160 had assembled a joint force from SEAL Team 6, the US Army's Delta Force, and C Company 1st/75th Rangers. SEAL Team 6 was assigned to capture the Beauséjour Radio Free Grenada transmitting station and Government House, hoping to rescue Sir Paul Scoon and his wife; Delta was to attack Richmond Hill Prison, while the Rangers were to secure Point Salines. The plan was for the JSOC troops to start their attacks by 0200 hours on 25 October, but this was completely wrecked by the decision to make 0500 hours the start time for the attack. This meant that the cover of darkness which would favour the attackers would largely be lost. This would prove to be a costly affair for the attacking Special Forces teams and the participants were well aware of the risks and tried to mitigate them within their resources. Lacking heavy support weapons, the would be at a significant disadvantage in the coming combat.[31]

In preparation for the attack, the US forces needed to position the helicopters from TF 160 closer to Grenada. There was no way that any such attack could be launched from the US. To that end, several C-5 Galaxies carried the two MH-6 Little Bird attack helicopters and the UH-60 Blackhawks of TF 160 to Barbados along with the men of SEAL Team 6 and the Delta Force and some of the Rangers. Nine UH-60s were earmarked for the operation, with three C-5s being assigned to transport them to Barbados where the aircraft would be assembled prior to their departure for Grenada at 0400 hours on 25 October. All nine UH-60s would depart Barbados together but two carrying SEALs would head for Beauséjour; two more, also with SEALs would head for Government House; and the other five, with Delta and Rangers aboard, would head for Richmond Hill Prison.[32]

The plan was for the helicopter-borne assault to arrive unexpectedly, relying on the element of surprise to give the attacking troops an initial advantage. A contested landing would be much more awkward for the attacking forces and given their lack of heavy equipment, be potentially disastrous.

Unfortunately, this was not to be the case. The helicopters of TF 160 had missed the night. They were approaching the north-eastern part of Grenada and with the Marines landing at Pearls and, as will be detailed later, the Rangers dropping at Point Salines, the Grenadians had been alerted to the attack and Radio Free Grenada was by now broadcasting frantic appeals for PRM members to report to their units and for international assistance to fight off the American attack. The delays occasioned by rushed planning and some bad luck had meant that the JSOC and TF 160 were 75 minutes late to their objectives.[33]

Fiasco at Beauséjour

The SEALS assigned to capture the radio station at Beauséjour had little difficulty. The Blackhawk helicopters were able to locate the radio station easily and only a few hundred metres from the beach, was easily identifiable by the large antenna. The guards on duty – no more than five – were overpowered and restrained. By 0630 hours the radio station had been secured. The SEALS were ordered to hold the station, not destroy it. However, the unit commander, Lieutenant Donald Erskine, chose an aggressive approach and deployed his men in ambush positions along the main road. One PRA soldier in a van was captured and joined his comrades in restraints. A PRM truck heading south to St. George's was ambushed with five of the militiamen being killed and the rest scattered. However, at 0930 hours, things changed for the worse for the SEALs.[34]

The PRAF had not been idle during this time. The RMC command at Fort Frederick organised two local counter attacks. The first of these was an operation to retake the radio station. At 0800 hours Lieutenant Prime was placed in command of a unit assigned to recapture the radio station. Then he sought out Lieutenant Raeburn Nelson. From Nelson, he was able to obtain a single BTR-60 APC, albeit released reluctantly, a rifle platoon of 20 PRA personnel from the mobile company with one 82mm mortar and its crew to provide fire support[35]. Transport for this ad hoc force was provided by a jeep, a van and a minibus. They arrived at the crest of the Happy Hill ridgeline with the station only 500 metres to the northeast. Prime then stopped to plan his attack using the forces at his disposal and the topography to the best advantage in the circumstances. He conceived a sound plan.

Prime positioned his mortar team on the ridge to provide fire support. The 15 solders in the civilian vehicles would dismount and move towards the perimeter of the building on foot and try to surround the radio station. The BTR-60, with Prime aboard, would continue towards the radio station, crossing the Beauséjour river bridge with the vehicle's heavy machine gun providing direct fire to oust the SEALS from the building.[36] Prime had appreciated that the SEALs would be lightly armed and as such, the PRA forces had a

Three A-7E Corsairs being catapulted from the bow of USS *Independence*. (Albert Grandolini Collection)

An A-7E from VA-87, high above Point Salines Airport. (US DoD)

The damage caused to several buildings of the Fort Frederick complex is clearly visible here. (US DoD)

significant firepower advantage over the American forces holed up in the station.

At around 0930 hours, Prime began his attack with the APC advancing across the bridge with its 14.5mm KPV machine gun firing at the building. The dismounted infantry went to ground and their supporting bipod-mounted PKM machine gun opened fire. The two machine guns, in particular the KPV, wrought havoc. The walls of the radio station offered no protection to the occupants. The SEALs had no anti-armour weapons. Attempts to call for air support were unsuccessful with no Spectre gunships being available to support the SEALs. After an hour, the SEALs withdrew from the station which was then successfully recaptured. The SEALs managed to hit the BTR-60 with a rifle-launched grenade, which disabled its turret. This gave Erskine and his men an opportunity to conduct a fighting withdrawal. Several SEALs, including Erskine were wounded in the firefight. The PRA had dislodged an elite SEAL team from its location and though it had suffered its own casualties, had achieved its assigned objective.

The dozen SEALs concealed themselves but an encounter with the PRA after dark convinced them to withdraw and swim back to the USS *Caron*, being picked up by a whale boat from the destroyer. The radio station was not allowed to resume broadcasting for very long. Air strikes by A-7s from the USS *Independence* silenced it but the antenna mast proved a stubborn target with the USS *Caron* firing some thirty 5-inch rounds at it without effect.

Prime and his men withdrew that evening, changed into civilian clothes and went into hiding as the US forces landed at Grand Mal, making their continued resistance completely untenable. However, his unit had performed well and this local PRA counterattack had been entirely successful.[37]

Prison Nightmare

The attack on the Richmond Hill Prison was an even bigger challenge than the attack on the Beauséjour radio station. Eight helicopters arrived over St. George's at 0615 hours in broad daylight. The Blackhawks carried cabin-mounted M60 machine guns for suppressing enemy infantry. However, they were faced with a withering crossfire from the PRA and PRM anti-aircraft units in St. George's. The Blackhawks, designated Chalks 1 through 8, planned to fly to a traffic circle in the middle of St. George's and then break off into two groups to assault the prison and Government House. Thanks to the heavy anti-aircraft fire, the turning point was missed. Chalk 4 saw its pilot, Captain Keith Lucas, hit in the arm and one of the door gunners, Specialist 4th Class Loren Richards, was hit in the leg. The eight aircraft headed out to sea to regroup. On the second approach, the two aircraft carrying SEALs – Chalk 7 and Chalk 8 – headed to their assigned mission at Government House.[38]

Chalk 4 after crashing at Amber Belair. (US National Archives)

Four UH-60As with different degrees of damage, seen at a collecting point after Operation Urgent Fury. (US National Archives)

An UH-60As of the 57th Medical Detachment, in the process of evacuating a casualty. (US DoD, via Albert Grandolini)

The remaining six Blackhawks headed to Richmond Hill Prison. As they flew through a valley leading to the prison, they were within range of the anti-aircraft guns based at Fort Frederick. Two M53 quad 12.7mm machine guns manned by the PRM plus two ZU-23-2 23mm guns manned by the PRA were firing at virtually point-blank range at the helicopters as they closed on Richmond Hill Prison. The soldiers of the PRA's security company, reinforced by prison guards, opened fire on the helicopters with their Kalashnikov rifles. Return fire from the M60 door gunners was joined by the Delta Force operators with their M177 carbines, targeting the anti-aircraft gunners with accurate, aimed, rifle fire to some effect.[39]

As the UH-60s swept in over the prison, two helicopters were then supposed to hover and allow teams from Delta's B squadron to 'fast rope' or rappel down to the ground. It was then that the irony of the situation became known. Richmond Hill Prison had been abandoned. The main gate of the prison and all the visible doors were wide open. The whole operation had been for nothing.[40]

The ordeal was not yet over. Aboard Chalk 4, Captain Lucas, already wounded, was killed when an anti-aircraft round exploded in his cockpit. The co-pilot, Chief Warrant Officer 2 Paul Price, was able to steer the crippled aircraft towards Point Salines which was now in the hands of the Rangers. As it passed the PRAF depot at Frequente, the two-gun ZU-23-2 PRA platoon based at the depot opened fire on the egressing helicopter. The now severely damaged machine crashed at Amber Belair, five kilometres south of St. George's.[41]

A second UH-60 was also severely damaged in the prison attack. Chalk 1 took a 12.7mm round through its floor, badly wounding Major William Boykin. No fewer than 53 additional 12.7mm rounds hit Chalk 1, wounding two other Delta operators and the pilot, Chief Warrant Officer 3 Bill Flannery.[42] Chalk 1 and the other Army helicopters were compelled to land aboard the USS *Guam* and other naval vessels. Despite the casualties among the Delta operators and the helicopter crews, those who were not wounded reboarded their helicopters and headed towards Point Salines, where they proceeded to support the Rangers who had parachuted in earlier that day.

While the helicopter pilots and the Delta operators had performed well as a team, one must ask questions about the planning of this operation. Delta operators underestimated the resistance they would face from the PRA and PRM. Many had opted not to wear neither helmets nor body armour.[43] No aircraft had been assigned to escort the vulnerable UH-60s. As the Marines noted at Pearls, Grenadian anti-aircraft fire was not something that could be easily ignored. If not for the AH-1T Sea Cobras, it is entirely possible that Marine losses at Pearls could have been quite significant. Surprisingly, no USAF AC-130s from the 16th Special Operations squadron were available to assist the TF 160 helicopter teams and while casualties were fortunately light, it was a stark reminder that the United States had seriously underestimated the intensity of PRAF resistance as well as its overall effectiveness.

Government House Chaos

If the SEALs at Beauséjour had been compelled to retreat in the face of a superior PRA force, those assigned to protect and evacuate Sir Paul Scoon and his household managed to find themselves besieged inside Government House. Sir Paul's household included some 11 people – his wife, his household staff and two policemen. One of the policemen was considered to be a RMC spy while the other, armed with an AK, was supposed to guard the main entrance.[44] The security of Sir Paul Scoon was of paramount importance as, in his capacity as Governor General, he was the closest thing left to a legitimate authority in Grenada. Already, thanks to a courtesy visit from the head of the RMC, General Hudson Austin, Sir Paul was aware of a possible invasion by the United States and was also told of the US warships known to be stationed off Grenada's shores. Operation Urgent Fury, therefore, is unlikely to have surprised Sir Paul. Needless to say, the sound of anti-aircraft fire from the nearby military installations and PRA troops alerted him to the US invasion.

Two helicopters from TF 160 were assigned to secure Sir Paul. The air mission commander, Major Robert Lee Johnson, was aboard one of the two Blackhawks. The aircraft carried the SEALs assigned to this task, the CIA Caribbean branch chief, a CIA radio operator who had a portable radio transmitter and Lawrence G. Rossin, a State Department political officer. These three civilians also carried a copy of the infamous undated draft letter for Sir Paul to sign to legitimise the invasion as being a requested military intervention. Rossin was nattily dressed, anticipating a photo opportunity with Sir Paul while the latter broadcast to Grenada in support of the US action. All of this presupposed that the landing at Government House would be unopposed. They were wrong.[45]

As a SEAL team dived out of one of the helicopters, they came under rifle fire from PRA troops. As the helicopter moved out of the line of fire, the anti-aircraft guns at Fort Frederick opened fire on it. The other passengers of the Blackhawk remained in the cabin as the helicopter tried to escape but as it did, the guns at Fort Rupert also engaged them. Johnson was hit in the leg and rendered unconscious while the co-pilot, Chief Warrant Officer 3 David Rosengrant, took over and was able to nurse the damaged helicopter to the USS *Guam*.[46]

So far, combat over Grenada had been less than auspicious for TF 160. Of the nine helicopters assigned to the operation, one had crashed on the island, another on the deck of the *Guam* and five more had been damaged sufficiently badly in combat that it was deemed that they needed repair. Only two were considered immediately combat capable. Of the 77 JSOC personnel and 45 aircrew aboard the nine aircraft, there had been one fatality (Lucas) with another 32 wounded in combat. It is a damning indictment of the Pentagon that these wounded are not 'officially acknowledged' in the list of casualties suffered during Operation Urgent Fury.[47]

Still, regardless of casualties and damage, there were SEALs at Government House with Sir Paul and his household to be rescued. The assault team, totalling two batches of 11 personnel each, was led by Lieutenant Wellington Leonard. These 22 men entered Government House and searched the premises for the Governor General. Sir Paul's driver opened the basement door and the SEALs were able to identify Sir Paul Scoon and his staff. The two policemen did not resist, though the one ostensibly guarding the gate was reluctant to surrender his rifle until his older colleague gently advised him to do so. While the SEALs secured the premises, the Governor General and his party were taken to the main dining

A disabled BTR-60PB outside Government House. (US National Archives)

Another view of the disabled and abandoned BTR-60PB that fought the SEALs. (US National Archives)

room where they could be both protected and shielded from the PRAF units that were all too ready to resist the US invasion.[48] The SEALs were very aware that PRAF installations were far too close to the official residences which were located on the hill known as Mount Wheldale. The PRA units at these installations were to effectively besiege the US troops in the mansion.[49]

Radio communication with the SEALs via hand-held MX-360 radios was seriously deficient and there were problems with effectively communicating and coordinating. The nominal SEAL commander, Captain (N) Gormly, could not get to the mansion, instead ending up at Point Salines where the JSOC units had established a command post. From there, they realised that the SEALs' radios could not communicate with USAF AC-130 gunships assigned to support them. As PRA troops launched a pincer attack on the mansion at around 1000 hours, undeterred by a conversation between the Grenadian police chief and Sir Paul Scoon, in which the latter sought to inflate US force numbers, the SEALs had to route their requests for air support through Army Delta Force operators.[50]

At 1015 hours, the first Spectre appeared over Government House. Its 20mm and 40mm guns shredded the PRA attackers. Shortly thereafter, another Spectre joined the first and together they put paid to the first attack. Another attack with two BTR-60s, after the two aircraft seemed to depart, were defeated when one of these Spectres returned and disabled one of the APCs.[51] During the attack by the APCs, Leonard had to call Fort Bragg from Sir Paul Scoon's telephone using a calling card. With this phone call, he was able to recall one of the Spectres in time to assist. Fighting degenerated into PRAF attacks against the defensive perimeter held by the 22 SEALs, six AC-130s rotating through attacks on the PRAF with Sir Paul's household taking cover on the floor of the mansion.[52] CPKF troops were able to assist the Spectres in targeting the PRA.

The JSOC troops were in dire need of assistance. Indeed, as will be shown, they needed to hold out until 0710 hours on 26 October – roughly a day – before troops of Golf Company of the 2nd Battalion/8th Marines were able to drive to the mansion and relieve the SEALs and secure Sir Paul Scoon, his wife and his household.[53]

Neutralising Fort Frederick

Admiral Metcalf was not happy about any of this as he had not been briefed about the JSOC operation and the importance of rescuing Sir Paul. He was then asked to relieve the besieged SEALs. This presented him with a major dilemma and was to result in a complete change of plan for the Americans to enable the diversion of sufficient forces to secure the Governor General and to relieve the SEALs who were under severe pressure from the PRAF.[54] One of the tasks which he was asked to perform in order to assist the SEALs was to neutralise the PRAF headquarters at Fort Frederick which was coordinating the attacks on the mansion, not to mention its role in defeating the American attack on Richmond Hill Prison and from where the PRA was preparing its operations. It was also quite well defended with anti-aircraft guns and would prove to be a difficult objective

A PRA ZU-23-2 gun deployed to cover Fort Frederick. (US National Archives)

An M53 quad barrelled 12.7mm AA machine gun. (US National Archives)

to take. However, taking Fort Frederick would effectively place the Americans in a completely dominant position in the entirety of St. George's. It had to be done.

Fort Frederick was a major challenge. It was located on the top of Richmond Hill, at a height of 750 feet. The fortifications were old, started by the French but completed by the British. It had never seen action in its roughly 200 years of existence – until now. If its fortifications were old, its defences, while sparse, were not insubstantial. The fort itself had a platoon of two ZU-23-2 guns from the PRA anti-aircraft battery. Other PRA guns, and M53 12.7mm guns from the PRM, were deployed at key positions throughout St. George's, all within line of sight of the PRA HQ.[55] The fort had a garrison of regular PRA troops, augmented by a few from the PRM. They were well-armed with assault rifles and machine guns and some RPGs. However, the garrison was relatively small, below company strength in effective capability.

An AH-1S Cobra of the US Army over Point Salines Airfield. (US National Archives)

Four Cobras and an OH-58 Kiowa of the US Army at a Forward Arming and Refueling Point. (US DoD, via Albert Grandolini)

Metcalf, understanding that an airstrike from the USS *Independence*'s air wing and its A-7 and A-6 attack aircraft was not feasible because of the location of the fort – in an urban area with a high risk of collateral damage – therefore eschewed the easy solution to neutralise the fort. Bombardment from naval 5-inch guns was also rejected for the same reason. This left but one option, the use of Marine AH-1T Sea Cobra attack helicopters. This was a reasonable option since the helicopters, with TOW ATGMs and 2.75-inch rockets in addition to 20mm cannon, could deliver precision firepower. However, there was the known risk that these helicopters were very vulnerable to AA fire and the ZU-23-2 guns would pose a major threat to the relatively lightly protected aircraft.

Nonetheless, two AH-1Ts, one commanded by Captain John Giguere and the other by Captain Timothy Howard, were routed from Point Salines.[56] Critically, they were not told of the AA defences at and around the fort. It was to prove to be a costly omission and would be one of many examples of the Americans underestimating the PRA and its resolve and its ability to effectively engage US aircraft and helicopters.

The two helicopters attacked the fort in tandem. Giguere marked the fort with a smoke rocket. His co-pilot/gunner Lieutenant Jeffery Scharver hit the fort with 2.75-inch rockets and 20mm cannon rounds. Howard, on the other hand, fired a TOW ATGM at the fort. On their fifth attack run, at 1327 hours, Howard's helicopter took at least three 23mm rounds. One hit the turbine and the other two hit Howard and his co-pilot Captain Jeb Seagle. Seagle was rendered unconscious while Howard had his right arm nearly severed and his right leg badly injured. The helicopter limped to a nearby sporting field where it crashed and started to burn. Seagle was able to drag the badly wounded Howard out of the helicopter and, after Howard threatened to shoot Seagle, the latter went to get physical help while Howard activated his emergency radio. Seagle was killed by PRA troops, some suggestions being that it was after he tried to surrender, but this cannot be confirmed.[57]

While Giguere's helicopter beat off PRA troops trying to capture Howard, a Marine CH-46E came in to try to rescue Howard. However, the PRA's AA guns in St. George's had only been partly silenced. One gun, to the north of Fort Rupert had been neutralised.

Another gun, defending Butler House, was a major threat to the rescue helicopter. It is possible that this gun was responsible for shooting down Howard's helicopter.

To ensure that the CH-46E would not face a similar fate, Giguere's Sea Cobra made repeated attacks on the gun position – many being complete bluffs as they were out of ammunition. However, the CH-46E successfully rescued Howard and the two helicopters turned to exit the scene. That was when the Sea Cobra was hit by AAA fire. It was a mortal wound to both the helicopter and the crew and the AH-1T went down into the ocean.[58] There were no survivors. The attack on Fort Frederick had failed. Two Sea Cobras had been shot down and three crewmen killed.

This fiasco let Metcalf to reconsider his approach to neutralise Fort Frederick and the AA batteries defending and covering St. George's. He consulted his land forces commander, Major General Schwarzkopf, and came to the conclusion that the use of air power was inevitable and that further delays could cause even more trouble. An airstrike on all of St. George's fortified positions, with particular emphasis on AA units was authorised and the A-7Es of the USS *Independence* were called in to launch a series of air strikes. By 1345 hours, the air strikes had achieved success, though not without civilian casualties, with 21 patients being killed when a 500 pound bomb hit Fort Matthew. The Americans thought it was another colonial fort used by the PRAF.[59] It was not, it was a psychiatric hospital and while its front entrance was clearly marked, there was no marking on its roof. It was a tragic event and could probably have been avoided had the Americans had better ground intelligence.

The Tanks Land

The level of abysmal US intelligence was compounded when they finally learned that there was a second university campus at Grand Anse. With the need to relieve the SEALs stuck in the Governor General's mansion as well as the need to secure the students at the second campus, the Americans decided on an amphibious landing at Grand Mal. Two Marine companies – Fox and Golf companies of the 2nd Battalion/8th Marines of the 22nd MAU were earmarked for this operation. Fox Company was supposed to ferried across the island by helicopter while Golf Company would land in 13 LTVP-7 amphibious assault tractors along with five M60A1 main battle tanks of A Company, 2nd Marine Tank Battalion. In addition, jeeps armed with TOW ATGMs and machine guns made up the accompanying units for Golf Company.[60]

At 1900 hours, 30 minutes late, the tanks and Golf Company made it to shore at Grand Mal, unopposed. This was fortunate as, landing on a very narrow area, the Marines could have been vulnerable to Grenadian or Cuban attack. In end, Metcalf and Schwarzkopf correctly calculated that the PRAF and their Cuban allies would be busy with the various American attacks elsewhere on the island.

The potential firepower and protection afforded by the M60A1s would have been intimidating to the PRA which had never engaged enemy armour before and had ageing weapons which were of dubious utility against main battle tanks. More importantly, in the 13 LTVP-7s, Golf Company was fully mobile and the force of 250 Marines was able to consolidate its position under cover of darkness – electricity now having been cut throughout the island and the

A USMC M60A1 tank in St. George's. (US National Archives)

Deck crew of the USS *Guam* using a fire hose to extinguish an engine fire on a UH-60A of the US Army. (US DoD)

PRA lacking night-vision equipment – and to secure their positions for an advance on the morning of 26 October. Fox Company after a number of hiccups, began to arrive by helicopter by 0400 hours on the 26th.[61]

Day One – The Cost

Against PRA and some Cuban resistance, the cost to the American forces might be deemed to be astonishingly high. Two AH-1T attack helicopters had been shot down, with three crewmembers killed. One UH-60 had been shot down and another so badly damaged that it crashed on the USS Guam. Five more had been damaged. Five Rangers were killed, adding to the two Rangers and four SEALs killed in parachute incidents. At least 36 more troops were badly injured.62

Of three key first day mission objectives – the radio station at Beauséjour, the rescue of Sir Paul Scoon and the rescue of US students – none were fully accomplished. On the other hand, both airports and the ports were under US control and with the arrival of Golf Company, the US had effectively opened a second front against ever diminishing PRA and Cuban resistance. 26 October promised to be much better for the Americans.

Day Two, 26 October 1983: Little Havana falls

The 2nd Brigade of the 82nd Airborne Division attacked towards the Cubans at Calliste and Little Havana early in the morning of 26 October 1983. A reconnaissance patrol led by Captain Ritz of Bravo Company, 2nd Battalion, 325th Infantry, was ambushed by Cubans, with Ritz and another soldier being killed and five wounded. The main attack against the Cubans started at about 0630 hours with the 82nd Airborne's artillery and Navy A-7s beginning a bombardment of the Cuban compound. Lacking AA guns, the Cubans were unable to stop the A-7s which made repeated passes, killing Cubans on each occasion. The defenders, few of whom were soldiers, moved from building to building as the 2nd Battalion attacked.[63]

An iconic image of US Army Rangers and troops of the 82nd Airborne Division moving out from Point Salines. (US National Archives)

The Cuban compound at Little Havana. (US National Archives)

Castro, in a display of utter callousness and with no grasp of reality, exhorted the Cubans to fight to the last man but neither Tortoló nor the rest of the few Cuban officers with him believed that such a course of action was either wise or fair to the construction workers under their command. After the fourth pass by the A-7s, the Cubans began to put white sheets in their windows. Bravo Company took control of the compound with tempers running high because of the casualties suffered by both sides. Some 16 Cubans were killed, including the diplomat Diaz, and 80 surrendered, of whom 29 were wounded. Bravo Company had suffered two dead and 10 wounded. Three, including Colonel Tortoló, escaped with the code books and other secret material to the Soviet embassy near Grand Anse. Little Havana was declared secure by 0835 hours on 26 October. Though the Americans did not know it, that was the end of Cuban resistance in Grenada.[64]

The 2nd Battalion headed towards the PRAF depot at Frequente from where the AA guns had engaged the Rangers on the first day. The depot was defended by a single sentry who wisely surrendered the entire depot. The haul was staggering – 6,322 rifles, perhaps dozens of 82mm mortars and ammunition, 13 AA guns, 15 recoilless rifles, 11 machine guns and 68 RPGs – and reflected the unfortunate

Cuban prisoners under guard at Point Salines. (US National Archives)

Troops of the 82nd Airborne Division on the move in St. George's. (US National Archives)

A knocked out BRDM-2 of the PRA. (US National Archives)

A famous photograph showing the apron of the Pearl Airport, with a C-130E of the USAF (foreground), next to a CH-46E of the US Marines, the 'captured' Cuban An-26 and the Grenadian An-2 in the background. (US DoD, via Albert Grandolini)

Lieutenant Frazer's inability to move anything more than a small proportion of the stores at Frequente.[65] It is also indicative of the absurd quantity of weapons procured by the PRG, way in excess of the needs of the PRAF, even if expanded. The loss of the depot at Frequente was a crippling blow to the PRAF and the RMC.

However, after they left the depot, a reconnaissance patrol of the 82nd Airborne ran into an ambush, allegedly from Cubans, but more likely from the PRA as the area was outside the Cuban defence zone. A BRDM-2 armoured car – a type used by the PRA's motorised company, not the Cubans on the island – was destroyed and four ambushers were killed. No casualties were suffered by US forces in combat in this operation but five soldiers were down with severe heat exhaustion in the heat of the tropical sun because of their heavy combat loads.[66]

Rescuing Scoon and the SEALs

Golf Company in its LTVP-7s and the five M60A1 tanks that accompanied them were finally joined by Fox Company which arrived by helicopter from Pearls via Point Salines. It took two hours for the company to land as only one helicopter could land at a time on the beach. Lieutenant Commander Ray Smith, CO of the 2nd Battalion/8th Marines, 22nd MAU, was able to assemble his force in pitch darkness but proceeded cautiously as he feared that he was being opposed by two battalions of PRA and Cuban troops. This was unnecessary as PRAF units were negligible and the Cubans entirely fictional.[67]

The 13 LTVP-7s and five M60A1s moved towards the capital, passing through a body of PRA soldiers who were deterred from any action by the presence of the tanks. The noise of the 18 tracked vehicles alone was enough to unnerve the PRAF troops who had never seen tanks, much less faced the prospect of having to fight them. The column arrived at the Queen's Park Racetrack at the northern edge of St. George's by 0430 hours. The Marines of Golf Company dismounted near the objective and, after establishing contact with the SEALs inside, they secured the PRA staging area at Bishop's residence, capturing a large quantity of weapons and equipment, including three trucks. Golf Company secured the Governor General's residence by 0710 hours and by 0900 hours, Sir Paul Scoon and his wife were flown to Point Salines where Brigadier Lewis of the BDF presented him with an identically worded batch of letters, backdated to 24 October and addressed to President Reagan and the Prime Ministers of Barbados, Jamaica and Dominica, requesting intervention. Sir Paul examined the letters, apparently made an alteration, and duly signed them without fuss.[68]

At this point, Sir Paul Scoon demonstrated his consummate political skill, despite not being a politician. Mr Rossin of the State Department encouraged Sir Paul to make a broadcast requesting intervention while presenting him with a list of names for a new interim government. Sir Paul refused to give the broadcast and also pointedly ignored the list of names. Instead, taking up temporary residence in the home of a friend, Scoon sought advice from Dr Vaughan Lewis, director general of the OECS and Buckingham Palace, on behalf of whom he acted. Sir Paul assumed the reins of power in Grenada and indicated that a 'vacuum of authority' existed that allowed him to take executive action. He effectively usurped the authority of the PRG and the RMC and restored Grenada's constitution with the ultimate aim of restoring a Westminster-style of democratic governance to the island.[69]

The RMC Flees

While Scoon was conducting his regime change operation with a pen, the RMC sought to save itself. Golf Company and the five M60A1s began to move towards Fort Frederick. Now that another day had come, PRAF resistance had begun to crumble. The tanks rumbling through St. George's, in particular, had scared the Grenadian leadership and they changed into civilian clothes and re-joined the general Grenadian population. On the path to Fort Frederick, two PRA armoured vehicles stood abandoned, one with its engines still running. By 1700 hours, Golf Company had entered the fort unopposed. Apparently, some PRA captives suggested that 16 Cuban officers had been at Fort Frederick until the morning of 26 October but this might have been unlikely, given Havana's orders and no evidence has been forthcoming, even after an all sources intelligence assessment led by the CIA.[70] However, despite the absence of Cuban advisors, the fall of Fort Frederick revealed a large quantity of munitions and weapons. These included three trucks full of AA ammunition, two trucks with three 82mm mortars and large numbers of assault rifles and machine guns. Of greater importance was the quantity of maps and documents obtained. The maps in particular showed all Grenadian military dispositions. Using these maps, Schwarzkopf planned to neutralise each one.[71]

Rescuing the Students at Grand Anse

The plan to rescue the students at Grand Anse was conceived to have three phases. In phase one, a Ranger assault force in Marine CH-46 helicopters would be flown in to establish a perimeter around the campus. Once secure, the heavy-lift CH-53 helicopters of the USMC would fly in to retrieve the students and final the CH-46s would return to extract the Rangers.[72]

The Rangers based at Point Salines had established telephone contact with the students at Grand Anse and, with a Resident Assistant from the True Blue campus, James Griffee, they were able to plan a reasonably coherent and workable plan to evacuate the students. The latter were to gather at 1200 hours on October 26 on the ground floor of a two-story students' residence building overlooking the beach. The students were able to inform the Rangers of PRAF dispositions in the area, including a M53 12.7mm quad machine gun stationed 500 metres northeast of the campus and the 15-20 PRAF soldiers located near the campus.[73]

Prior to the evacuation, AC-130s and A-7s joined 82nd Airborne's mortars and artillery in bombarding suspected PRAF and Cuban positions. The latter were non-existent, and much attention was spent on attacking the Carifta cottages only because they were leased to Cuban engineers working on the Point Salines runway. The old Police Training College was also attacked although most students believed it to be a roofless former hotel. The sole M53 AA gun fired a few rounds before being silenced by return fire from a Spectre gunship.

At 1630 hours, nine CH-46 helicopters in three flights of three aircraft approached and disgorged the Rangers. One managed to get itself entangled with some palm fonds and ended up being damaged, though it was declared flyable. However, the Rangers were able to quickly secure the perimeter. The CH-53s were not

A CH-46E (AerNo 157654) of HMM-261 on the ground in Grenada. (US DoD)

82nd Airborne Division 105mm M101 howitzers in action. (US National Archives)

The wreck of the USMC CH-46 lost during the rescue of the students, seen after being destroyed by an AC-130H gunship. (US National Archives)

US troops with a 60mm mortar. (US National Archives)

and picked up by the destroyer USS *Caron*. The students had been successfully evacuated with only five Rangers being wounded but with one CH-46 wrecked and another damaged. Fortunately, no students were injured in this operation. Another 200 US students, living off campus, were reached the next day without incident while 21 other students never left Grenada.[75]

At a cost of two dead and under two dozen wounded, the Americans had secured all their key objectives. The students, at least all those who could be easily reached, were rescued, Sir Paul Scoon had taken over as a civilian constitutional authority, and Cuban resistance had ended with the fall of Little Havana. More importantly, with USMC tanks entering St. George's, the RMC and PRAF leadership had abandoned their weapons depot and HQ, crippling their ability to resist.

long in coming and taking in some 50 passengers each; in all, five CH-53s evacuated 233 civilians to Point Salines. Three others – Dr Robert Jordan, a histology instructor hampered by a leg brace and a German Shepherd named Brandy – hid in the Spice Island Hotel where the following morning they encountered troops of the 82nd Airborne Division.[74]

Extracting the Rangers, however, proved to be not quite so easy. As the CH-46s returned, bombs from 82mm mortars began landing around the helicopters. One CH-46 made contact with a palm tree and a tree trunk fell onto the rotor blades, wrecking the helicopter. With two of the nine CH-46s assigned to the Rangers out of action, 11 Rangers of Charlie Company were left behind. They had planned to evade and avoid the PRA and to link up with the 82nd Airborne. However, concerned about friendly fire in the dark, the Rangers decided to use the rubber life rafts aboard the wrecked CH-46 to row out to the naval vessels off-shore. They were spotted

Day Three, 27 October 1983

By Thursday, 27 October, the PRA had started to fall apart. As has been mentioned above, the PRAF leadership – Austin, James and Layne – had escaped Fort Frederick early on the morning of 26 October. The PRA began to melt away with soldiers changing into civilian clothes and, like Second Lieutenant Raeburn Nelson, returned to their respective homes to await arrest. For the leaders, however, escape from Grenada was essential if they were to survive.

Arming themselves with Makarov pistols, a single AK and grenades and with USD 7,000 in cash, the three military leaders sought assistance from an East German, Gerhard Jonas, to secure a yacht to take them to safety. While awaiting this, they hid in

UH-1N helicopter of HMM-261 coming in to land. Notable is the door gunner with his pintle-mounted M60 machine gun. (US National Archives)

Aerial bombardment of PRA positions on Point Calivigny. (US DoD)

an abandoned bungalow facing Westerhall Bay. However, Major Hartland of the BDF and Lieutenant Commander Tomlin of the RSS had guessed their plan and Hartland and Tomlin set out in a captured GAZ jeep with a US soldier as an escort. They were able to find out the location of Austin, James and Layne. Though they were discovered, capture was not possible. It was not until 30 October that the three were captured, a full five days after their escape from Fort Frederick.[76]

While the PRAF leadership was planning their escape, the Americans planned an assault on the Calivigny military barracks. In a complete overestimation of the possible opposition, the US Rangers were told to expect a full battalion of the PRA as well as 300 to 400 Cuban military advisors along with 60 Soviet specialists. This overestimation of Cuban and Soviet presence in Grenada was a feature of American planning and early reporting during Operation Urgent Fury. This unfortunately extended into casualty reporting where PRAF soldiers killed, captured or wounded were all too often identified as Cuban. In the case of those killed, this meant that roughly three times the number of Cubans actually killed in action were reported by US troops.

A flight of UH-60s. (US National Archives)

US troops boarding a UH-60 helicopter. (US National Archives)

The operation was prepared with only 15 minutes notice and it showed. Bombardment from 17 105mm howitzers from three batteries of artillery attached to the 82nd Airborne lobbed 500 shells at Calivigny, most of which fell into the sea. An aerial bombardment by A-7s from the Navy and an AC-130 destroyed many buildings, apparently clearing the way for the Rangers.[77] The camp at Calivigny was almost completely destroyed by the airstrikes, with its fuel depots destroyed and the buildings completely demolished. On the other hand, there was virtually no resistance as, contrary to US expectations, the camp was virtually deserted and the claimed presence of a battery of six ZU-23-2 AA guns was a complete fallacy with not a single AA gun firing in defence of the camp. Yet, the Americans planned for the worst. They got it, though not in the way they expected.

In four flights of four UH-60s each, with each helicopter carrying 15 men, the Rangers approached. The first two helicopters landed easily but the third, possibly hit by ground fire from the few desultory rounds fired by the PRA, went down and landed violently, bouncing towards another UH-60. The two helicopters collided and tore their rotors off.

Another Blackhawk tried to avoid the two wrecks and landed hard. After disgorging its Rangers, this helicopter tried to get airborne but its landing had caused it severe damage and it crashed, right in the mist of the Rangers. Three Rangers were killed; Private Lannon, Sergeant Slater and Private Grenier. Three more Rangers were badly wounded and Sergeant Sears was left permanently paralysed from the incident.[78] Little resistance was encountered and few PRAF troops were in the vicinity.

This third day of Urgent Fury was rounded out by an unfortunate friendly fire incident when a Combat Support Company attached to the 2nd Brigade of the 82nd Airborne came under sniper fire. A newly arrived Air and Naval Gunfire Liaison Officer called in an airstrike of one Navy A-7 aircraft. This aircraft made a strafing run – right into the command post of the 2nd Brigade. Seventeen members of the Brigade staff were wounded, with one later succumbing to his wounds.[79] Blue-on-Blue incidents caused all the casualties suffered this day.

Day three was a fiasco. A tragedy of errors and accidents. However, it was also evident that there was increasingly little organised resistance to the Americans and the end of the operation was nigh. The RMC and the PRA leadership were rendered completely ineffective and the PRAF had virtually collapsed.

Day Four, 28 October 1983

With resistance collapsing and the feared Cuban-led guerrilla movement being a complete myth, operations began to wind down. The fear of a guerrilla campaign caused the Americans to waste much time looking for Cubans where none existed. The Cubans had either surrendered or fled. None were in a position to offer any resistance and with the PRAF destroyed, deserted or disintegrated, there was not any chance that any armed opposition would be encountered. As the Cubans were rounded up and the PRA and PRM surrendered or were turned in by the compatriots, it was evident that combat operations were at an end.

It should be noted that while Austin and his two colleagues were holed up in a house near the coast, the hunt for Bernard Coard ended somewhat sooner when he, his wife and Strachan were identified as living in a private house on the outskirts of St. George's. On Saturday, 29 October, Marines of the 22nd MAU persuaded them to surrender when they turned an anti-tank weapon on the house.

Coard, the last to emerge, kept repeating 'I am not responsible'. After being held by the Americans for eight days, the Coard and Austin groups were taken to Richmond Hill Prison where they were charged in the civilian criminal courts for the murder of Bishop and his supporters on 19 October.[80]

The last military operation took place on 1 November, after most operations had ceased. On that day, Marines staged a sea and helicopter landing on the island of Carriacou anticipating to either find Cubans or a large cache of weapons. They found 19 PRA soldiers who surrendered without a fight.

Operation Urgent Fury was finally over.

US troops on the move in Grenada. (US National Archives)

US troops in St. George's. One carries an M47 Dragon ATGM. (US National Archives)

7
CONCLUSION

Operation Urgent Fury was over. The United States had succeeded in ousting the RMC and Sir Paul Scoon had established an interim government which wasted no time in expelling the Soviet and Cuban embassies, after disarming those with weapons – the latter being because of an anti-aircraft gun mounted on the roof of the Soviet embassy which may have fired on US aircraft. Grenada would get a new start as a functioning, Westminster-style democracy. Cuba, in particular, suffered a major loss in prestige and influence as well as financially.[1] They suffered a further setback when the dictator of Suriname – Desi Bouterse – asked the Cubans to leave, explicitly citing the Grenada invasion as his prime motivation.[2] On the other hand, the Soviets reconciled themselves quickly to Sir Paul Scoon's government despite condemning the US action as vociferously as possible.

Reaction to the US invasion was predictable, being generally not favourable with the UN and the Commonwealth heads of government reacting negatively. Reaction from Canada and the UK was also not favourable with the latter being particularly piqued at Reagan's failure to inform Prime Minister Thatcher in a timely manner. The British were angry and humiliated but ultimately, the relationship between Reagan and Thatcher smoothed over any discomfiture that might have temporarily existed.

The Cost

Casualties suffered by all sides in Grenada are not entirely clear. The number of US dead is relatively easy to calculate with 19 known fatalities – 12 from the Army (eight from the Rangers and three from the 82nd Airborne plus one pilot), three from the USMC and four from the Navy. The wounded, however, are far less easy to calculate as 'reportable wounded' excluded casualties among the SEALs, TF 160 and the Delta Force. Of the known wounded, 108 were from the Army, 15 from the USMC, and two from the Air Force. This may not account for all the wounded either as using some estimates, just based on the casualties sustained by JSOC and TF 160 personnel, the total would go from 125 to 157. If US 'Purple Heart' medals are to be taken into account, then 219 US servicemen were wounded in the Grenada operation.[3]

The US lost no vehicles to hostile action but its helicopter losses were high – nine were destroyed or severely damaged. Of these, at least three were shot down and the others were badly damaged in collisions or encounters with vegetation. In addition, several helicopters received damage from AA fire of a less serious nature with five UH-60s of TF 160 being affected. Of 32 UH-60s deployed, one was shot down and six badly damaged with another five being lightly damaged. One CH-46E was destroyed (out of 12 deployed) and two AH-1s (out of four deployed) were shot down. Out of a total of 107 helicopters deployed by the US, nine were lost and perhaps another half a dozen received minor damage.[4] Given the fact that

A member of the USAF Security Police in front of an Ilyushin Il-62 airliner that collected Cuban citizens from Grenada after Operation Urgent Fury. (US DoD)

Fidel Castro greets Colonel Tortolo on his return to Cuba. (US National Archives)

the PRAF had only light anti-aircraft weapons with no advanced sighting systems, these losses look substantial, but it should be noted that the losses seem to have been as a result of the US seriously underestimating the PRAF.

Set against this must be set Cuban casualties of 25 killed and 59 wounded. Only two of the Cubans killed and eight of the wounded were professional soldiers, reflecting the fact that only 43 Cuban soldiers were on the island. The US tried to return the bodies of some 68 killed to Cuba, but most of these turned out to be PRAF personnel. Unfortunately, the ordeal for the Cubans did not end with their eventual return to Cuba in November 1983. The CIA reported in a 1984 'All Sources' intelligence assessment that Castro was not pleased with the lack of vigour of the Cuban defensive effort. Those not wounded were demoted or reprimanded. Colonel Pedro Tortoló Comas was demoted to the rank of private and sent to Angola. In 1986 he was killed in an ambush set up by UNITA against a joint Cuban-Angolan MLPA convoy.[5] To call Castro's attitude repulsive is to be kind. Given 17 hours to prepare and completely outgunned and outmanned and fighting for a RMC with no legitimacy, the Cubans had no incentive to fight, and Castro's own orders hampered their deployment. The treatment of the Cuban soldiers who fought in Grenada was disgraceful.

The Grenadian PRAF, however, suffered some 45 dead. The force had done most of the fighting and had, overall, performed commendably. Its arsenal was completely lost when Operation Urgent Fury ended. At least 24 Grenadian civilians were killed, some 21 of them when the psychiatric hospital was bombed in error. It is believed that 358 Grenadians were wounded but this is not broken down between PRAF and civilians and there is much confusion in differentiating the two.[6] That is a large number of wounded for the tiny size of the PRAF that resisted the US invasion and the fact that, in the main, the US took care under its rules of engagement to minimise civilian casualties.

Grenada Recovers

To call Grenada a mess after the US invasion would be an understatement. The economy was a shambles, many buildings had been destroyed in the fighting, though Grenada was far from an urban wasteland after combat ceased. Critically, however, there was now a lack of security. The US and CPKF troops maintained a degree of public order but with large numbers of weapons unaccounted for and PRAF personnel now unemployed, the potential for trouble was there. Looting in the immediate aftermath of the invasion was widespread with even Lady Scoon – Sir Paul's wife – not being spared, having all her jewellery stolen. Allegations abounded of heavy-handed search operations by US troops that were, in the main, unfounded.

The US troops, in particular, were keen to withdraw and after a few months, the majority were withdrawn. Remaining on the island were 250 US military specialists, including 30 from the US Special Forces who stayed behind to assist in training the Grenadian police. Most of these last US troops were withdrawn by June 1985. In addition, 100 Jamaican and Barbadian soldiers and police remained behind to assist in this task and to aid in re-establishing a viable police presence on the island with a competent Grenadian police force.[7]

To deal with the latter point, the United Kingdom helped to rebuild the demoralised RGPF with the able assistance of other Caribbean police forces, most notably Barbados. Though compelled, out of necessity, to accept former PRA and PRM personnel as recruits, despite the initially questionable loyalty and reliability of such recruits. The RGPF emerged as a force that was able to control Grenada's internal security situation and did so without usually carrying firearms. The military was never to re-emerge in any discernible form, with the RGPF taking over that role with an 80-man SSU and a 30-person Coast Guard. The transition to a civilian police force was accomplished with remarkably little trouble and with considerable efficiency.

Politically, Sir Paul Scoon moved, on 15 November 1983, to establish an interim government with a nine-member Advisory Committee overseeing the transition back into a democratic form of government. Grenadians were tired, in 1983, of any political discourse and focused their attention on rebuilding their lives and livelihoods at a time of economic downturn in the region. The United States was generous with economic assistance, however, and Grenada was able to regain its economic equilibrium. Even Point Salines Airport was eventually completed with American assistance.[8]

Elections were eventually held on 3 December 1984 and for a while it looked like the old Prime Minister Eric Gairy and his GULP would be re-elected. Pro-Bishop supporters – Einstein Louison, Radix, Gahagan and others – formed the Maurice Bishop Patriotic Movement (MBPM) and fought hard against Gairy. However, the US could not allow Gairy or the MBPM to win. So, with the assistance of Tom Adams of Barbados, the New National Party (NNP), led by Herbert Blaize, Gairy's arch-rival before independence, was formed.

Sir Paul Scoon addressing the press on the forming of the interim government. (US National Archives)

There was no contest. In the December 1984 elections, Blaize's NNP won 14 of the 15 seats.[9] In a twist of fate, as this book is being written, the NNP, under Keith Mitchell is currently in power in Grenada with a supermajority of 15 of 15 seats.

Justice Served?

In mid-November 1983, Richmond Hill Prison was becoming full. The RMC's leaders and those responsible for Bishop's death were held within. Initially, the filthy prison was practically being run by the inmates. However, the arrival of senior Barbadian Prison officer Lionel Maloney changed all of that. With the able support of the JDF rifle platoon assigned to guard the prison, Maloney restored the morale of the prison staff and instilled a sense of discipline in the prisoners. Infractions were punished and despite allegations of torture against the Barbadian police team investigating and preparing the evidence against the accused, no evidence was ever found to substantiate such allegations. [10]

There were also two escape attempts – one by Coard's wife, Phyllis, which failed and another, much more serious, which allegedly involved caches of PRAF weapons and an attempt to assassinate or take hostage prison and Barbadian police officials and to destroy US helicopters. It was taken very seriously when a vehicle carrying Layne, Redhead, James and others outside the Grenville courthouse, found itself accosted by ex-PRA Officer Cadet, Ronnie Spooner. He threatened a Jamaican corporal and was nearly shot. On him was correspondence intended for the prisoners. With his arrest, the plot came to an end.[11]

Finally, on 4 December 1986, after an eight-month trial, the verdicts were handed down. Bluster from the Coards, abuse from Abdullah and revolutionary rhetoric from Layne and James did not deter the St. Kitts born Chief Justice, Dennis Byron. Fourteen were sentenced to hang – Austin, the Coards, Layne, Stroude, Prime, Strachan, Abdullah and Redhead among them. Three others from Bishop's execution squad – Mitchell, Joseph and Richardson – received lengthy prison sentences. Police Commissioner Ian St. Bernard escaped prosecution for want of evidence and Sergeant Fabian Gabriel was similarly fortunate. One man was acquitted – Raeburn Nelson. Fortune had placed him in that third APC and Caribbean justice, while mind-numbingly slow at times, is neither capricious nor cruel.[12]

That would seemingly have been the end. However, the death sentences were commuted to life in prison in 1991. In 2007, the Judicial Committee of the Privy Council examined the sentences and commuted them still further to 30 years, with time already served being taken into account. Between 2008 and 2009, Coard and the others, were released. Coard and Layne later wrote books – the former writing three volumes – which, while intellectually very interesting, showed neither remorse nor regret about what they had done.

A Last Word

Operation Urgent Fury has occasionally been portrayed as a fight against global communism and as an operation to liberate a Caribbean island from Cuban domination. This is not without truth but is a complete exaggeration. The US invasion of Grenada was born out of an opportunity gifted to the United States and the pro-Western states of the OECS, Jamaica and Barbados, to remove a Marxist regime which had lost all legitimacy. Coard and his cohorts, in their lust for power and their cruelty, perpetrated a massacre of Grenadian civilians at Fort Rupert as well as the murder of Prime Minister Bishop and others. This action opened the path to US intervention.

In 1979, Bishop took power with much goodwill. Four years later, a grab for power led to his murder. The PRG betrayed the idealism of 1979 but the RMC turned betrayal into tragedy.

BIBLIOGRAPHY

Books and Articles

Adkin, M., *Urgent Fury: The Battle for Grenada* (London: Leo Cooper, 1989)

Bolger, D.P., 'Operation Urgent Fury and Its Critics', *Military Review* (July 1986), pp.60–69

Cole, R.H., *Operation Urgent Fury: Grenada 1983* (Washington D.C.: Joint History Office, 1997)

Conway's All the World's Fighting Ships (London: Conway Maritime Press, 1995)

Conway's All the World's Fighting Ships 1947–1995 (London: Conway Maritime Press, 1995)

Grenada, a Preliminary Report (Washington D.C., United States Department of Defence: December 16 1983)

Grenada: October 25 to November 2 1983 (Washington D.C.: U.S. Department of Defence, 1983)

Interagency Intelligence Assessment 19 December 1983 – Grenada: A First Look at Mechanisms of Control and Foreign Involvement

Joint History Office, Office of the Chairman of the Joint Chiefs of Staff, *Operation Urgent Fury* (CreateSpace Independent Publishing Platform, 2014)

Layne, J.E., *We Move Tonight: The Making of the Grenada Revolution* (Grenada Revolution Memorial Foundation, 2014)

Kukielski, P., *The U.S. Invasion of Grenada: Legacy of a Flawed Victory* (Jefferson: McFarland & Co, 2019)

Operation Urgent Fury (Columbia: Center of Military History, 2021)

Phillips, Dion E., 'The Creation, Structure and Training of the Barbados Defense Force', *Caribbean Studies*, Vol. 21, No. 1/2, (1988), pp. 124–157

Raines E.F. Jr., *The Rucksack War* (Washington D.C.: Center of Military History United States Army, 2010)

Russell, Lee E. & Albert Mendez, M., *Grenada 1983* (London: Osprey, 1983)

Sandford, G.W., *The New Jewel Movement: Grenada's Revolution 1979–1983* (Washington D.C.: Foreign Service Institute, Department of State, 1985)

Smith, G., *The Assassination of Maurice Bishop* (Kingston: Ian Randler Publishers, 2020)

Web Articles and Sites

'13 March 1979, Radio Free Grenada, Maurice Bishop, Address to the Nation', *The Grenada Revolution Online*, <https://www.thegrenadarevolutiononline.com/page1.html> accessed 11 January 2022

'1st District Jamaica Defence Force Coast Guard', *Jamaica Defence Force Official Website*, <https://www.jdfweb.com/1st-dist-jdf-coast-guard/>

'About the Barbados Coast Guard', *Barbados Defence Force*, <https://www.bdfbarbados.com/the-barbados-coast-guard/>

'About Us', *Regional Security System*, <https://www.rss.org.bb/about-us/>

'All-Time Aircraft Used List Jamaican Defence Force', *Aeroflight.co.uk*, <http://www.aeroflight.co.uk/user/every/jamaica-df-all-time-aircraft-used-listing.htm>

'Barbados Defence Force', *Aeroflight.co.uk*, <http://www.aeroflight.co.uk/ops/mil/barbados-defence-force.htm>

'BLOODY MONDAY, or the "Battle of St. George's" 21 January 1974', *Grenada Revolution Online* <https://www.thegrenadarevolutiononline.com/bloodymonday.html> accessed 11 January 2022

'CVW-6 (AE): Dec.20 1963 – Apr.1. 1992', <http://www.gonavy.jp/CVW-AEf.html> accessed 14 January 2022

'Grenada: Operation Urgent Fury', *Naval History and Heritage Command*, <https://www.history.navy.mil/research/library/online-reading-room/title-list-alphabetically/g/grenada-operation-urgent-fury.html> accessed 14 January 2022

'Jamaica Defence Force', *Aeroflight.co.uk*, <http://www.aeroflight.co.uk/ops/mil/jamaican-defence-force.htm>

'Jamaica Regiment', *Global Security.org, <https://www.globalsecurity.org/military/world/caribbean/jm-regiment.htm>*

'JDF to Acquire New Fleet of Armoured Vehicles', *Jamaica Information Service* (3 December 2013) <https://jis.gov.jm/jdf-acquire-new-fleet-armoured-vehicles/>

'The Manifesto of the New Jewel Movement', *The Grenada Revolution Online*, <https://www.thegrenadarevolutiononline.com/manifesto.html> accessed 11 January 2022

'U.S. and Allied Forces for Operation Urgent Fury: The Invasion of Grenada 1983', <https://www.fireandfury.com/orbats/modgrenadaus.pdf>

'What About the Cubans?', *The Grenada Revolution Online*, <https://www.thegrenadarevolutiononline.com/page4.html> accessed 13 January 2022

'What Was the PRA, PRAF and PRM?" T*he Grenada Revolution Online*, <https://www.thegrenadarevolutiononline.com/page2c.html> accessed 11 January 2022

Long, W.R., 'Last of U.S. Troops Leave Grenada : 30 Americans Stay to Train Caribbean Nation's Police', *L.A. Times* (12 June 1985) <https://www.latimes.com/archives/la-xpm-1985-06-12-mn-6111-story.html> accessed 31 January 2022

Miller, P., 'New Documents Reveal Britain's Secret Plan to Invade a Tiny Caribbean Island', *Vice.com* (24 October 2014) <https://www.vice.com/en/article/3b74yb/revealed-britains-top-secret-plan-to-invade-a-tiny-caribbean-island> accessed 11 January 2022

Silverstone, S.A., 'Intervention and Use of Force', *Oxford Bibliographies*, (2 March 2011) <https://www.oxfordbibliographies.com/view/document/obo-9780199743292/obo-9780199743292-0047.xml> accessed 12 January 2022

Taylor, C., '1951 And The Coming Of First General Elections On The Basis Of Universal Adult Suffrage', *Big Drum Nation*, (1 August 2008) <https://web.archive.org/web/20200801065517/http://www.bigdrumnation.org/comments/1stgeneralelection.html> accessed 11 January 2022

Taylor, C., 'From Old Representative System To Modified Crown Colony And The Elections Of 1925', *Big Drum Nation*, (1 August 2008) <https://web.archive.org/

web/20200801080545/http://www.bigdrumnation.org/comments/crowncolony.html> accessed 11 January 2022

NOTES

Chapter 1

1 S.A. Silverstone, 'Intervention and Use of Force', Oxford Bibliographies (2 March 2011), <https://www.oxfordbibliographies.com/view/document/obo-9780199743292/obo-9780199743292-0047.xml> (Accessed 12 January 2022).
2 Fedon was the son of a French jeweller and a freed black slave.
3 C. Taylor, 'From Old Representative System To Modified Crown Colony And The Elections Of 1925', *Big Drum Nation* (1 August 2008), <https://web.archive.org/web/20200801080545/http://www.bigdrumnation.org/comments/crowncolony.html>, accessed 11 January 2022.
4 C. Taylor, '1951 And The Coming Of First General Elections On The Basis Of Universal Adult Suffrage'.
5 G. W. Sandford, *The New Jewel Movement: Grenada's Revolution 1979-1983* (Washington D.C.: Foreign Service Institute, Department of State, 1985), pp.4–8.
6 Mark Adkin, *Urgent Fury: The Battle for Grenada* (London: Leo Cooper, 1989) pp.5–7.
7 'The Manifesto of the New Jewel Movement', The Grenada Revolution Online <https://www.thegrenadarevolutiononline.com/manifesto.html>, accessed 11 January 2022.
8 'Bloody Monday, or the "Battle of St. George's, 21 January 1974', Grenada Revolution Online <https://www.thegrenadarevolutiononline.com/bloodymonday.html>, accessed 11 January 2022.
9 'Bloody Monday, or the "Battle of St. George's, 21 January 1974', Grenada Revolution Online.
10 'Bloody Monday, or the "Battle of St. George's, 21 January 1974', Grenada Revolution Online.
11 'Bloody Monday, or the "Battle of St. George's, 21 January 1974', Grenada Revolution Online.
12 P. Miller, 'New Documents Reveal Britain's Secret Plan to Invade a Tiny Caribbean Island', Vice.com (24 October 2014) <https://www.vice.com/en/article/3b74yb/revealed-britains-top-secret-plan-to-invade-a-tiny-caribbean-island>, accessed 11 January 2022.
13 'What Was the PRA, PRAF and PRM?', The Grenada Revolution Online <https://www.thegrenadarevolutiononline.com/page2c.html>, accessed 11 January 2022.
14 J.E. Layne, *We Move Tonight: The Making of the Grenada Revolution* (Grenada Revolution Memorial Foundation, 2014), p.52.
15 'What Was the PRA, PRAF and PRM?', The Grenada Revolution Online <https://www.thegrenadarevolutiononline.com/page2c.html>, accessed 11 January 2022.
16 'What Was the PRA, PRAF and PRM?', The Grenada Revolution Online.
17 Sandford, *The New Jewel Movement: Grenada's Revolution 1979–1983*, pp.37–40.
18 Sandford, *The New Jewel Movement: Grenada's Revolution 1979–1983*, pp.37–40.
19 Sandford, *The New Jewel Movement: Grenada's Revolution 1979–1983*, pp.37–40.
20 '13 March 1979, Radio Free Grenada, Maurice Bishop, Address to the Nation', The Grenada Revolution Online <https://www.thegrenadarevolutiononline.com/page1.html>, accessed 11 January 2022.

Chapter 2

1 Adkin, *Urgent Fury*, pp.10–11.
2 Adkin, *Urgent Fury*, pp.12–14.
3 Adkin, *Urgent Fury*, pp.16–17.
4 Adkin, *Urgent Fury*, p.19.
5 Adkin, *Urgent Fury*, pp.17–18.
6 Adkin, *Urgent Fury*, p.18.
7 Adkin, *Urgent Fury*, p.18.
8 Adkin, *Urgent Fury*, p.20.
9 *Interagency Intelligence Assessment 19 December 1983 – Grenada: A first look at Mechanisms of Control and Foreign Involvement*, p.7.
10 *Interagency Intelligence Assessment 19 December 1983 – Grenada: A first look at Mechanisms of Control and Foreign Involvement*, p.7–10.
11 *Interagency Intelligence Assessment 19 December 1983 – Grenada: A first look at Mechanisms of Control and Foreign Involvement*, p.7–10.
12 *Grenada, a Preliminary Report* (Washington D.C.: United States Department of Defence, December 16 1983), p.5.
13 *Interagency Intelligence Assessment 19 December 1983- Grenada: A first look at Mechanisms of Control and Foreign Involvement*, pp.12–13.
14 *Interagency Intelligence Assessment 19 December 1983 – Grenada: A first look at Mechanisms of Control and Foreign Involvement*, p.11–12.
15 *Interagency Intelligence Assessment 19 December 1983 – Grenada: A first look at Mechanisms of Control and Foreign Involvement*, p.9.
16 *Interagency Intelligence Assessment 19 December 1983 – Grenada: A first look at Mechanisms of Control and Foreign Involvement*, pp.9–12.
17 Adkin, *Urgent Fury*, pp.28–32.
18 Adkin, *Urgent Fury*, pp.35–39.
19 Adkin, *Urgent Fury*, pp.35–39.
20 Adkin, *Urgent Fury*, pp.35–39.
21 Adkin, *Urgent Fury*, pp.35–39.
22 G. Smith, *The Assassination of Maurice Bishop*, (Kingston: Ian Randler Publishers, 2020) pp.85–91.
23 Smith, *The Assassination of Maurice Bishop*, pp.82–91.
24 Smith, *The Assassination of Maurice Bishop*, p.92.
25 Smith, *The Assassination of Maurice Bishop*, p.94.
26 Smith, *The Assassination of Maurice Bishop*, p.98.
27 Smith, *The Assassination of Maurice Bishop*, pp.101–105.
28 Smith, *The Assassination of Maurice Bishop*, pp.106–107.
29 Smith, *The Assassination of Maurice Bishop*, pp.109–110.
30 Adkin, *Urgent Fury*, pp.44–45.
31 Adkin, *Urgent Fury*, pp.44–45.
32 Adkin, *Urgent Fury*, pp.44–45.
33 Smith, *The Assassination of Maurice Bishop*, pp.131–134.
34 Smith, *The Assassination of Maurice Bishop*, pp.136–138.
35 Smith, *The Assassination of Maurice Bishop*, pp.136–138.
36 Smith, *The Assassination of Maurice Bishop*, pp.136–138.
37 Smith, *The Assassination of Maurice Bishop*, pp.139–140.
38 Adkin, *Urgent Fury*, pp.59–61.
39 Smith, *The Assassination of Maurice Bishop*, pp.144–145.
40 Adkin, *Urgent Fury*, pp.64–67.
41 Adkin, *Urgent Fury*, pp.64–67.
42 Smith, *The Assassination of Maurice Bishop*, pp.144–148.
43 Smith, *The Assassination of Maurice Bishop*, pp.144–148.
44 Smith, *The Assassination of Maurice Bishop*, p.147.
45 Smith, *The Assassination of Maurice Bishop*, p.151.
46 Adkin, *Urgent Fury*, pp.74–75.
47 Adkin, *Urgent Fury*, pp.74–75.
48 Adkin, *Urgent Fury*, p.76.
49 Adkin, *Urgent Fury*, p.76.

Chapter 3

1 Adkin, *Urgent Fury*, pp.96–100.
2 Adkin, *Urgent Fury*, pp.96–100.
3 Adkin, *Urgent Fury*, p.98.
4 Adkin, *Urgent Fury*, p.98.
5 Adkin, *Urgent Fury*, p.117.
6 Adkin, *Urgent Fury*, p.118.
7 Adkin, *Urgent Fury*, pp.100–102.
8 Adkin, *Urgent Fury*, pp.100–102.
9 Adkin, *Urgent Fury*, p.113.
10 Adkin, *Urgent Fury*, p.99.
11 Adkin, *Urgent Fury*, p.99.
12 Adkin, *Urgent Fury*, p.114.
13 Adkin, *Urgent Fury*, p.115.

14 P. Kukielski, *The US Invasion of Grenada: Legacy of a Flawed Victory,* (Jefferson: McFarland & Co, 2019) p.73.

Chapter 4

1 E.F. Raines, Jr., *The Rucksack War,* (Washington D.C.: Center of Military History United States Army, 2010) p.76.
2 Raines, Jr., *The Rucksack War,* p.76.
3 Raines, Jr., *The Rucksack War,* p.79
4 'U.S. and Allied Forces for Operation Urgent Fury: The Invasion of Grenada 1983' <https://www.fireandfury.com/orbats/modgrenadaus.pdf>
5 'U.S. and Allied Forces for Operation Urgent Fury: The Invasion of Grenada 1983' <https://www.fireandfury.com/orbats/modgrenadaus.pdf>
6 'Grenada: Operation Urgent Fury', *Naval History and Heritage Command,* <https://www.history.navy.mil/research/library/online-reading-room/title-list-alphabetically/g/grenada-operation-urgent-fury.html>, accessed 14 January 2022.
7 'CVW-6 (AE): Dec.20 1963 – Apr.1. 1992, <http://www.gonavy.jp/CVW-AEf.html>, accessed 14 January 2022.
8 'U.S. and Allied Forces for Operation Urgent Fury: The Invasion of Grenada 1983', <https://www.fireandfury.com/orbats/modgrenadaus.pdf>
9 'U.S. and Allied Forces for Operation Urgent Fury: The Invasion of Grenada 1983', <https://www.fireandfury.com/orbats/modgrenadaus.pdf>
10 D.P. Bolger, 'Operation Urgent Fury and Its Critics', *Military Review,* (July 1986), pp.60–69.
11 Bolger, 'Operation Urgent Fury and Its Critics', pp.60–69.
12 Adkin, *Urgent Fury: The Battle for Grenada,* p.219.
13 'Interview With Former Arms Dealer, Mercenary Leader', *The Weekend Nation,* (3 Feb 84), pp.16-17.
14 Dion E. Phillips, 'The Creation, Structure and Training of the Barbados Defense Force', *Caribbean Studies, Vol. 21,* (No. 1/2, 1988), p.134.
15 'About the Barbados Coast Guard', *Barbados Defence Force,* <https://www.bdfbarbados.com/the-barbados-coast-guard/>
16 *Conway's All the World's Fighting Ships,* (London: Conway Maritime Press, 1995), p.24.
17 'Barbados Defence Force', *Aeroflight.co.uk,* <http://www.aeroflight.co.uk/ops/mil/barbados-defence-force.htm>
18 'Jamaica Regiment', *Global Security.org,* <https://www.globalsecurity.org/military/world/caribbean/jm-regiment.htm>
19 'Jamaica Regiment', *Global Security.org,* <https://www.globalsecurity.org/military/world/caribbean/jm-regiment.htm>
20 'Jamaica Regiment', *Global Security.org,* <https://www.globalsecurity.org/military/world/caribbean/jm-regiment.htm>
21 'Jamaica Regiment', *Global Security.org,* <https://www.globalsecurity.org/military/world/caribbean/jm-regiment.htm>
22 'Jamaica Regiment', *Global Security.org,* <https://www.globalsecurity.org/military/world/caribbean/jm-regiment.htm>
23 'Jamaica Regiment', *Global Security.org,* <https://www.globalsecurity.org/military/world/caribbean/jm-regiment.htm>
24 'JDF to Acquire New Fleet of Armoured Vehicles', *Jamaica Information Service,* (3 December 2013), <https://jis.gov.jm/jdf-acquire-new-fleet-armoured-vehicles/>
25 'Jamaica Defence Force', *Aeroflight.co.uk,* <http://www.aeroflight.co.uk/ops/mil/jamaican-defence-force.htm>
26 'Jamaica Defence Force', *Aeroflight.co.uk,* <http://www.aeroflight.co.uk/ops/mil/jamaican-defence-force.htm>
27 'Jamaica Defence Force', *Aeroflight.co.uk,* <http://www.aeroflight.co.uk/ops/mil/jamaican-defence-force.htm>
28 'All-Time Aircraft Used List Jamaican Defence Force', *Aeroflight.co.uk,* <http://www.aeroflight.co.uk/user/every/jamaica-df-all-time-aircraft-used-listing.htm>
29 '1st District Jamaica Defence Force Coast Guard', *Jamaica Defence Force Official Website* <https://www.jdfweb.com/1st-dist-jdf-coast-guard/>
30 '1st District Jamaica Defence Force Coast Guard', *Jamaica Defence Force Official Website* <https://www.jdfweb.com/1st-dist-jdf-coast-guard/>
31 *Conway's All the World's Fighting Ships 1947–1995,* (London: Conway Maritime Press, 1995), p.219.
32 'About Us', *Regional Security System,* <https://www.rss.org.bb/about-us/>
33 Lee E. Russell & M. Albert Mendez, *Grenada 1983,* (London: Osprey, 1983), pp.5–7 and pp.45–46.
34 Joint History Office, Office of the Chairman of the Joint Chiefs of Staff, *Operation Urgent Fury,* (CreateSpace Independent Publishing Platform, 2014) p.36.
35 Raines, *The Rucksack War,* p.356.
36 'What Was the PRA, PRAF and PRM?', *The Grenada Revolution Online,* <https://www.thegrenadarevolutiononline.com/page2c.html>, accessed 13 January 2022.
37 'What Was the PRA, PRAF and PRM?', *The Grenada Revolution Online.*
38 Raines, *The Rucksack War,* p.16–21.
39 Raines, *The Rucksack War,* p.16–21.
40 Raines, *The Rucksack War,* p.16.
41 Raines, *The Rucksack War,* pp.16–17.
42 Raines, *The Rucksack War,* p.17.
43 Raines, *The Rucksack War,* p.19.
44 Raines, *The Rucksack War,* p.20.
45 Raines, *The Rucksack War,* p.18.
46 Adkin, *Urgent Fury,* p.24.
47 *Grenada, a Preliminary Report* (Washington D.C.: United States Department of Defence, December 16 1983), p.23.
48 *Interagency Intelligence Assessment 19 December 1983 – Grenada: A First Look at Mechanisms of Control and Foreign Involvement,* p.10.
49 *Grenada, a Preliminary Report,* p.24.
50 '3. Captured Weapons and Equipment from Grenada', *Grenada: October 25 to November 2 1983,* (Washington D.C.: US Department of Defence, 1983), p.15.
51 Raines, *The Rucksack War,* p.168.
52 'What About the Cubans?' *The Grenada Revolution Online,* <https://www.thegrenadarevolutiononline.com/page4.html>, accessed 13 January 2022.
53 Raines, *The Rucksack War,* p.170.
54 Adkin, *Urgent Fury,* p.162.
55 *Interagency Intelligence Assessment 19 December 1983 – Grenada: A First Look at Mechanisms of Control and Foreign Involvement,* p.14.
56 Raines, *The Rucksack War,* p.23.

Chapter 5

1 R.H. Cole, *Operation Urgent Fury: Grenada 1983* (Washington D.C.: Joint History Office, 1997), pp.6–7.
2 Cole, *Operation Urgent Fury: Grenada 1983*, pp.1–2.
3 Adkin, *Urgent Fury,* p.126.
4 Adkin, *Urgent Fury,* p.126.
5 Cole, *Operation Urgent Fury: Grenada 1983,* pp.23–24.
6 Cole, *Operation Urgent Fury: Grenada 1983*, p.19–21.
7 Cole, *Operation Urgent Fury: Grenada 1983*, p.19–21.
8 Cole, *Operation Urgent Fury: Grenada 1983*, pp.24–25.
9 Cole, *Operation Urgent Fury: Grenada 1983*, pp.26–28.
10 Cole, *Operation Urgent Fury: Grenada 1983*, p.34.
11 Cole, *Operation Urgent Fury: Grenada 1983*, pp.28–29.
12 Cole, *Operation Urgent Fury: Grenada 1983*, pp.65–67.
13 D.P. Bolger, 'Operation Urgent Fury and Its Critics', *Military Review,* (July 1986), pp.57–69.
14 Cole, *Urgent Fury,* p.34.
15 Adkin, *Urgent Fury*, p.92.
16 Adkin, *Urgent Fury*, pp.92–93.
17 Adkin, *Urgent Fury*, pp.92–93.
18 Adkin, *Urgent Fury*, pp.92–93.
19 Adkin, *Urgent Fury*, pp.92–93.
20 Adkin, *Urgent Fury*, p.93.
21 Adkin, *Urgent Fury*, p.94.
22 Adkin, *Urgent Fury*, pp.94–95.
23 Adkin, *Urgent Fury*, pp.94–95.
24 Adkin, *Urgent Fury*, pp.129–130.
25 Adkin, *Urgent Fury*, p.219.
26 Raines, *The Rucksack War*, p.22.
27 Raines, *The Rucksack War*, p.23.
28 Adkin, *Urgent Fury,* pp.162–163.
29 Adkin, *Urgent Fury*, p.164.
30 Adkin, *Urgent Fury*, p.164.
31 Adkin, *Urgent Fury*, p.164.
32 Adkin, *Urgent Fury*, pp.164-165.
33 Adkin, *Urgent Fury*, pp.164-165.
34 Adkin, *Urgent Fury*, p.165.
35 Raines, *The Rucksack War*, p.169.
36 Adkin, *Urgent Fury,* pp.160–161.
37 Raines, *The Rucksack War,* p.170.
38 Raines, *The Rucksack War,* p.170.
39 Raines, *The Rucksack War,* pp.165–166.
40 Raines, *The Rucksack War,* p.166.

Chapter 6

1 Kukielski, *The US Invasion of Grenada,* pp.40–45.
2 Kukielski, *The US Invasion of Grenada,* pp.40–45.
3 Kukielski, *The US Invasion of Grenada,* pp.40–45.
4 Kukielski, *The US Invasion of Grenada,* pp.40–45.
5 Kukielski, *The US Invasion of Grenada,* pp.40–45.
6 Kukielski, *The US Invasion of Grenada,* pp.40–45.
7 Adkin, *Urgent Fury,* pp.193–198.
8 Adkin, *Urgent Fury,* pp.193–198.
9 Adkin, *Urgent Fury,* pp.193–198.
10 Adkin, *Urgent Fury,* pp.200–204.
11 Adkin, *Urgent Fury,* pp.200–204.
12 Adkin, *Urgent Fury,* pp.205–207.
13 Adkin, *Urgent Fury,* p.209.
14 Adkin, *Urgent Fury,* pp.213–217.
15 Adkin, *Urgent Fury,* pp.213–217.
16 Adkin, *Urgent Fury,* pp.213–217.
17 Adkin, *Urgent Fury,* p.225.
18 Adkin, *Urgent Fury,* p.225.
19 Adkin, *Urgent Fury,* pp.216–218.
20 Adkin, *Urgent Fury,* pp.223–228.
21 Adkin, *Urgent Fury,* p.219.
22 Adkin, *Urgent Fury,* p.219.
23 Adkin, *Urgent Fury,* p.228.
24 Kukielski, *The US Invasion of Grenada,* pp.117–120.
25 Kukielski, *The US Invasion of Grenada,* pp.117–120.
26 Kukielski, *The US Invasion of Grenada,* pp.117–120.
27 Adkin, *Urgent Fury,* pp.219–222.
28 Adkin, *Urgent Fury,* p.220.
29 Adkin, *Urgent Fury,* p.220.
30 Adkin, *Urgent Fury,* p.221.
31 Adkin, *Urgent Fury,* pp.175–180.
32 Adkin, *Urgent Fury,* pp.175–180.
33 Adkin, *Urgent Fury,* pp.179–180.
34 Adkin, *Urgent Fury,* pp.181–182.
35 Adkin, *Urgent Fury,* pp.181–183.
36 Adkin, *Urgent Fury,* pp.181–183.
37 Adkin, *Urgent Fury,* pp.181–183.
38 Kukielski, *The US Invasion of Grenada,* pp.60–68.
39 Kukielski, *The US Invasion of Grenada,* pp.60–68.
40 Kukielski, *The US Invasion of Grenada,* pp.60–68.
41 Kukielski, *The US Invasion of Grenada,* pp.60–68.
42 Kukielski, *The US Invasion of Grenada,* pp.60–68.
43 Kukielski, *The US Invasion of Grenada,* p.60.
44 Kukielski, *The US Invasion of Grenada,* p.74.
45 Kukielski, *The US Invasion of Grenada,* pp.74–75.
46 Kukielski, *The US Invasion of Grenada,* pp.74–75.
47 Kukielski, *The US Invasion of Grenada,* pp.75–76.
48 Kukielski, *The US Invasion of Grenada,* p.93.
49 Kukielski, *The US Invasion of Grenada,* pp.93–95.
50 Kukielski, *The US Invasion of Grenada,* pp.93–95.
51 Kukielski, *The US Invasion of Grenada,* pp.93–95.
52 Kukielski, *The US Invasion of Grenada,* pp.93–95.
53 Kukielski, *The US Invasion of Grenada,* p.104.
54 Kukielski, *The US Invasion of Grenada,* pp.95–97.
55 Kukielski, *The US Invasion of Grenada,* pp.95–98.
56 Kukielski, *The US Invasion of Grenada,* pp.95–98.
57 Kukielski, *The US Invasion of Grenada,* pp.95–98.
58 Kukielski, *The US Invasion of Grenada,* pp.95–98.
59 Kukielski, *The US Invasion of Grenada,* pp.95–98.
60 Kukielski, *The US Invasion of Grenada,* pp.99–101.
61 Kukielski, *The US Invasion of Grenada,* pp.99–101.
62 Kukielski, *The US Invasion of Grenada,* p.103.
63 Kukielski, *The US Invasion of Grenada,* pp.120–123.
64 Kukielski, *The US Invasion of Grenada,* pp.120–123.
65 Kukielski, *The US Invasion of Grenada,* pp.120–123.
66 Kukielski, *The US Invasion of Grenada,* pp.120–123.
67 Kukielski, *The US Invasion of Grenada,* pp.103–106.
68 Kukielski, *The US Invasion of Grenada,* pp.103–106.
69 Kukielski, *The US Invasion of Grenada,* pp.103–106.
70 Kukielski, *The US Invasion of Grenada,* pp.103–106.
71 Kukielski, *The US Invasion of Grenada,* pp.103–106.
72 Kukielski, *The US Invasion of Grenada,* pp.108–113.
73 Kukielski, *The US Invasion of Grenada,* pp.108–113.
74 Kukielski, *The US Invasion of Grenada,* pp.108–113.
75 Kukielski, *The US Invasion of Grenada,* pp.108–113.
76 Adkin, *Urgent Fury,* pp.293–298.
77 Kukielski, *The US Invasion of Grenada,* pp.126–128.
78 Kukielski, *The US Invasion of Grenada,* pp.126–128.
79 Kukielski, *The US Invasion of Grenada,* p.130.
80 Kukielski, *The US Invasion of Grenada,* p.133.

Chapter 7

1 Kukielski, *The US Invasion of Grenada,* pp.155–158.
2 Kukielski, *The US Invasion of Grenada,* pp.192–193.
3 Kukielski, *The US Invasion of Grenada,* pp.157–159.
4 Adkin, *Urgent Fury,* p.357.
5 Adkin, *Urgent Fury,* pp.314–316.
6 Kukielski, *The US Invasion of Grenada,* pp.158–159.
7 W.R. Long, 'Last of U.S. Troops Leave Grenada : 30 Americans Stay to Train Caribbean Nation's Police', *L.A. Times* (12 June 1985), <https://www.latimes.com/archives/la-xpm-1985-06-12-mn-6111-story.html>, accessed 31 January 2022.
8 Adkin, *Urgent Fury,* pp.323–326.
9 Adkin, *Urgent Fury,* pp.323–326.
10 Adkin, *Urgent Fury,* pp.326–329.
11 Adkin, *Urgent Fury,* pp.326–329.
12 Adkin, *Urgent Fury,* pp.330–331.

ABOUT THE AUTHOR

Sanjay **Badri-Maharaj**, from Trinidad, received his MA and PhD from the Department of War Studies, Kings College London. His thesis was on India's Nuclear Weapons Program. He has written and published extensively, including four books – *The Armageddon Factor: Nuclear Weapons in the India-Pakistan Context* (2000) and *Indian Nuclear Strategy: Confronting the Potential Nuclear Threat from both Pakistan and China* (2018) and a number of titles for Helion's various @War series. He is an attorney-at-law and has served as a consultant to the Ministry of National Security in Trinidad and was a Visiting International Fellow at the Institute for Defence Studies and Analyses in New Delhi.